Advance Praise for
Build a Culture of Good

Build a Culture of Good is more than a book. It's the story of how Scott Moorehead and Ryan McCarty set out to create a foundation where employees had permission to care about their customers, their communities, and each other. The lessons contained in the book will help any organization that cares about its people and its purpose to learn how to make a positive difference in the world. Compelling as well as entertaining, *Build a Culture of Good* is a book for anyone who dares to challenge the status quo as a means of ensuring a better tomorrow.

> — **JOHN BALDONI**, global chair, Leadership Development, N2Growth Inc. Top 50 Leadership Expert, and author of more than a dozen books on leadership

I've never seen two men who are more giving, selfless, and caring than Ryan McCarty and Scott Moorehead. The powerful duo has worked for years to make the Culture of Good something that others can identify and practice within their own companies. This book tells the story of not only a growing business but also the journey to build and foster a genuine culture of good in a workplace.

> — **CRYSTAL KADAKIA**, modern workplace and millennial expert, keynote speaker, and author two-time TEDx speaker | Power 30 under 30

Build a Culture of Good is a book for our times. It provides proof and a reminder that income and impact need not be mutually exclusive. Highly recommended.

> — **RAJESH SETTY**, cofounder of Audvisor, author of *Gratitude* and a dozen other books

What Ryan and Scott have done for TCC through the Culture of Good is simply outstanding: they have unlocked one of the key tenets of employee loyalty, tapping their desire to help others and be of service. One of the qualities of being a Small Giant is giving back to the community, not just because it is the right thing to do but because it is also good for the business. Establishing a sustainable community program is no easy task, and Ryan and Scott have done just that with the Culture of Good. If you have the opportunity to learn how they do it, run; don't walk. That's why their book *Build a Culture of Good* is so incredible—it teaches you how you can create your own Cultures of Good within your companies.

> — **PAUL SPIEGELMAN**, CEO of Small Giants Community

Congratulations to TCC. They've been honored with Stevie Awards, and now they tell their inspiring story in this moving book.

> — **MICHAEL GALLAGHER**, president of the Stevie Awards

The tools and insights Scott and Ryan share in their book are visionary. Just as with TCC, Riley Children's Foundation is "For the Kids." Not only does TCC raise the bar for corporate philanthropy but also it is an innovator in delivering the importance and value behind the commitment to making a difference to the members of the community, its customers, and its team members.

> — **KEVIN O'KEEFE**, president and CEO, Riley Children's Foundation

BUILD A CULTURE OF GOOD

UNLEASH RESULTS BY LETTING YOUR EMPLOYEES BRING THEIR SOUL TO WORK

SCOTT MOOREHEAD | RYAN MCCARTY

Foreword by MARSHALL GOLDSMITH

Executive coach, business educator, and *New York Times* best-selling author, ranked no. 1 leadership thinker in the world by Thinkers50

Culture of Good, Inc.
Carmel, IN

Published by
Culture of Good, Inc.
Carmel, IN

Publisher's Cataloging-in-Publication Data
Moorehead, Scott.
    Build a culture of good : unleash results by letting your employees bring
    their soul to work / Scott Moorehead and Ryan McCarty. – Carmel, IN : Culture of
    Good, Inc., 2017.

    p. ; cm.

    ISBN13: 978-0-9980094-0-7

    1. Employee motivation. 2. Management—Employee participation.
    3. Personnel management. 4. Corporate culture. I. Title.
    II. McCarty, Ryan.

HF5549.5.M63 M66 2017
658.314—dc23   2016953586

Project coordination by Jenkins Group, Inc.
www.BookPublishing.com

Interior design by Brooke Camfield

Printed in the United States of America
21   20   19   18   17   •   5   4   3   2   1

Dedicated to each TCC employee who has taken their permission to care and built an amazing Culture of Good.

Contents

Foreword

Companies spend billions trying to boost employee engagement: that elusive, idealized condition in which workers are "in the zone," to borrow a phrase from sports. When people are engaged, they are committed, interested, active, productive—in short, they care.

As an executive coach and a business educator, I have spent years grappling with why this idea is so hard to instill in some people. To put it simply: how do you get people to care? In *Build a Culture of Good*, Scott and Ryan show how a philanthropic mission that is deeply connected to every facet of the organization is good for customers, employees, and the community. I find this approach compelling for many reasons—not least because it offers a new perspective on how to motivate and engage employees.

Of course, many companies have mission statements focused on good works or high ideals. At the vast majority of these companies, however, mission statements are engraved onto plaques, hung on the wall, and promptly forgotten. Scott and Ryan are suggesting a fundamentally different approach: weaving the mission into the company's core activities so that employees know exactly how their work is connected to specific charitable outcomes—real people who get real help.

Scott and Ryan are onto something here. Doing good is of course worthwhile for its own sake. I challenge you to stay dry-eyed as you read about the lives affected by these wonderful charitable activities. Think of all the people who will benefit if more companies adopt this approach! But it's also a smart business strategy to pull an entire organization, its customers, and its community together around projects with authenticity and purpose.

A common cause—whatever it happens to be—can be transformative. Paul O'Neill knew this when he made worker safety the top priority at aluminum manufacturer Alcoa in the late 1980s. Everyone began communicating in a new way, efficiency improved, and profits skyrocketed. Giving underserved kids backpacks stuffed with school supplies—as Scott and Ryan did at TCC—is another type of catalyst for improved performance across the board.

It's a lot harder to be cynical or hostile in a company whose culture is deeply identified with doing good works. Nobody can legitimately gripe, "What does this all mean, anyway?" Instead, employees have every reason to be professional and committed—a mind-set that is key to engagement. My daughter, Dr. Kelly Goldsmith, who has a PhD from Yale in behavioral marketing and teaches at Northwestern's Kellogg School of Management, has given me some valuable insight into this idea.

Kelly and I have spent hours talking about why employee engagement efforts so often backfire. The first symptom, she told me, is the employee engagement survey. These typically contain almost exclusively *passive* questions, such as, "Do you receive helpful feedback from your manager?" or "Do you feel that the organization values the contribution you make?" Essentially, they are asking about the environment around the employee and how it can be improved so that the employee will be happier and work more productively.

Let me be clear: there is nothing wrong with these questions. They provide companies with a lot of valuable information. But they are by nature diagnostic, not curative, casting employees as passive recipients of company policies or programs. They prompt employees to look at external factors such as the incompetence of their manager or the disorganization of their surroundings—not themselves. They are ignoring half of the equation: the employee's responsibility for his or her behavior (and his or her happiness). Rather than an added burden, this kind of responsibility is liberating and empowering. Think of it this way: what really makes you feel better about your job, getting a special perk or succeeding at a worthy and challenging task?

That's why I suggest that companies should ask active questions as well as the usual passive ones. For example, instead of "Did you set clear goals?" they should try asking "Did you *do your best* to set clear goals?" Instead of "Were you engaged in your work today?" they should ask "Did you *do your best* to be engaged in your work today?"

To test whether active questions really do improve engagement, Kelly and I initiated a controlled study in which we measured employees' outlook following a training program. The results were even better than we expected. The control group showed little change. The passive questions group reported positive improvement—but the active questions group doubled that improvement on every item! Active questions were twice as effective at delivering training's desired benefits to employees.

Every day, I ask myself 43 of these active questions—which cover whether I did my best to be a good husband, exercise, and meet my other priorities in life. These Daily Questions, as I call them, make me take active responsibility for the things I care about most. They ensure that I am focused more on what I give than what I get.

Build a Culture of Good takes this principle to its logical conclusion. If work is less about passive getting and more about active giving, everyone wins.

Marshall Goldsmith
Executive coach, business educator, and *New York Times* best-selling author, ranked no. 1 leadership thinker in the world by Thinkers50

Introducing the
Culture of Good

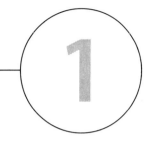

Do you think there's something magical about chips and salsa (other than how delicious they are)? We do! These two ingredients seem to be what it took to change the culture in our business and to create what we think is the most unique corporate operating system on the planet: the Culture of Good. The seeds of what we've come to call our Culture of Good movement, which is what this book is all about, were planted over many discussions involving chips and salsa. As you read on, you might want to grab some chips and salsa for yourself as we share our story.

One of us, Ryan McCarty, was a practicing pastor, and the other, Scott Moorehead, is CEO of TCC, a thriving telecommunications firm with more than 800 stores and 3,000 employees. However, our true identities might be hard to guess when you take a first gander at us. Ryan is what you could call edgy: funky glasses, tattoos, earrings, and a manly beard. He ain't your father's pastor. Scott, who is partial to the jam band Phish, is clean-shaven but has the mouth of a sailor. Be warned: the pages that follow will contain some mild profanity. For example, Scott has been known to conclude his company-wide talks with his patented phrase: "Namaste, bitches."

We both come from Marion, Indiana, a small rural town just over an hour north of Indianapolis. But it wasn't until we met up at a Mexican restaurant that we really got to know each other. What we recognized almost immediately was that we had chemistry, something you might see between two brothers. While we look different on the outside and often approach issues from a differing point of view, we also share something deep inside our cores.

Think about what happens when you have two electrical wires. On their own, they look ordinary enough. But when you cross those live wires, ZAP! You get sparks.

The day our wires first crossed came in June 2012, about a week before we met up for chips and salsa. It was at God's House, the church that Ryan and his wife, Katara, had started on their own a decade or so before in their home in Marion. Just like he did almost every Sunday, Ryan was sharing his sermon with the 300 or so folks who had shown up for the service.

As it happened, Scott was sitting in a pew in that auditorium with his wife, Julie, and his kids that day. His parents had been going to God's House for about a year, and, for some reason, Scott decided to bring his family along that Sunday. That was something, because, as Scott admits, he's not that into church. But there he was, in the audience, when Ryan got up and started sharing his message.

But rather than throwing around fire and brimstone, Ryan was talking about something inspirational: he was asking why we do what we do. "If our why isn't bigger than our what," Ryan said before he had ever heard of Simon Sinek, who popularized a similar theme with his book *Start with Why*, "we can become discouraged regardless of what we are doing in our lives. So what is your why? And does it equal your what?"

2

Strangely enough, this was the second time Ryan had given this particular sermon—which made it the one and only time he ever repeated a sermon of any kind. Was that some kind of divine sign? Ryan would probably say yes. Scott, eh. The important point was that the message of having your why equal your what struck Scott right where it counted: his heart.

At that time, Scott was running the company his parents had founded a few decades before. He was young and ambitious and had put the company on a fast track of growth. The wireless business was booming, and TCC was positioned to ride right to the top of the industry.

Or was it?

Scott had begun to wonder what it was that motivated him and his employees. The company was growing rapidly and expanding geographically away from its original nucleus. The challenge of running the business was that it had stopped becoming a mom-and-pop shop. The threat was that it would lose the identity that got it to where it was. If you run a small company that is tied closely together, getting everyone motivated and headed in the same direction is an easier task. But as you grow, challenges occur in getting everyone headed the same way for the same reason.

The management style at TCC had always considered the feelings of the employees first. Scott calls this the third dimension of leadership. Many managers make two-dimensional decisions. Those two dimensions are the X- and Y-axes of the lines that make up spreadsheets. Behind those calls are easy decisions that take no real art or soul. The business was at a turning point where less of the third dimension seemed to be happening, and Scott wanted it back.

Now, here was this funky pastor talking about your why equaling your what. Scott was intrigued. Check that—he was inspired. He wanted to know more about this guy.

Later on, Scott asked his parents whether they had Ryan's phone number. They did. So he called Ryan, introduced himself, and invited him to lunch later that week. And that's when those two wires connected— ZAP!—over a basket of tortilla chips and salsa. Magic ensued.

Scott talked about how inspiring Ryan's message had been and how he was hoping to bring more of the why back into his business. "Our company already does so much good, but our employees don't know it," Scott said. "We cut checks to organizations all the time, but nobody gives a damn about it. Maybe you can help mentor me to help the employees understand the why behind this." Scott then asked Ryan about how he and his wife ran their church.

"We started with four people, and now we have nine employees," Ryan told him. "Our mission is simple: we inspire people to go out and do good. We call it making uncommon love common."

"I want to figure out how to inspire people in my business," Scott replied. "If the employees would be inspired more, then the customers would be inspired. Imagine if we did that in every city we serve. It would go beyond the employees. It would impact communities, hundreds of thousands of people. That's some Tony Robbins kind of shit right there!"

With that, Scott pulled out a pen and began to draw a figure on a napkin. "It's like a circle that feeds itself," he said. "The more our employees care, the more customers will be drawn to us. And the more customers who choose to do business with us, the more we can give back to our communities. It's a virtuous circle of success!"

As he sat there munching chips and listening to this potentially crazy Phish-head, the more Ryan was blown away. He knew Scott's folks a bit, but he was clueless until then as to what they did or that Scott was running a billion-dollar business with thousands of employees.

But the more he listened to Scott and the kind of impact he wanted to make on his employees and in the community through his business, the more excited he became. Every week he tried his best to make an impact on the lives of the 300 parishioners who showed up each Sunday. Imagine what might happen if he could help inspire thousands of TCC employees. Even better, what would happen when those employees were empowered to go out into their local communities and do as much good as they possibly could?

"I have an idea," Ryan told Scott. "You should hire me."

Scott did eventually hire Ryan, but that's another story for later.

A Culture of OK versus a Culture of Good

We've written this book as a way to chronicle our journey together in changing a corporate culture without a plan and building a new operating system dubbed the Culture of Good, or COG. But, to be frank, when we started this, we didn't even really know what a company "culture" was. "I used to think if you had culture, it meant you drank your coffee with your pinkie in the air," says Scott. But we've evolved that definition over time. Now, we define culture as what most of your people are doing most of the time inside your organization as it relates to your norms, beliefs, and values. Or, to put that another way, your culture is the true secret sauce that sets your organization apart from every other organization. "I believe that no matter what your company sells, no matter what it does, no matter how many inventions or patents you have, the one thing that nobody can steal is your culture," says Scott.

This movement that became the operating system was founded on the basis that if we did the right things for the right reasons, our employees and customers would agree and we would all win. We have learned that when you encourage your employees to bring their hearts and minds—their souls, if you will—to work with them on a daily basis, amazing things happen. Little did we know that by setting out to do the right things for the right reasons, we would create a system that would not only give us a competitive advantage in our business but also fuel our growth and success.

We have learned that you don't have to separate doing good from doing your job because they are one and the same: that you give as much as you get. It's what we call "the give equaling the take." When you give people the permission to care at work, you can change the world.

We have learned that great employees can inspire your customers, and having a common cause shared by both is paramount. That's the secret sauce. It's never doing those three components in silos but rather doing them all at once.

But don't take that the wrong way either. We recognize that most companies out there give back in some way. Corporate social responsibility programs, or CSRs, as they're called these days, have become all the rage. If you own a business, perhaps you cut a check at the end of the year to help out a few nonprofit organizations. Or, maybe, if you work for a progressive-minded boss, he or she gives you the chance to volunteer while you're still on the clock. You might even find ways to do all of the above away from the office on your own time, which is absolutely a noble thing to do.

The challenge we've taken up in our business in partnership with the people we work with is to think about doing good as more than just a series of "programs" or corporate-sponsored initiatives. What's missing is that when you label something this way, it makes it feel forced, fake, inauthentic, or even somehow incomplete. Be honest: how enthusiastic are all of you about that latest CSR program you have in place at the office? Are you truly passionate about the belief that in doing your job every day, you are doing real good? How do we take those moments of generosity and turn them into a movement that inspires contagious passion not just in our communities and among our employees but also with our customers? Or, to put that another way, **how can we take what might be a**

decent-enough organizational culture, which you might call a Culture of OK, and transform it into a Culture of Good?

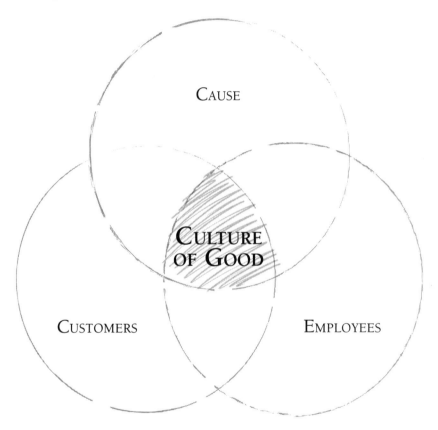

We've been indoctrinated to the notion that the nonprofit and for-profit worlds are not only separate from each other but also at odds with each other. We've been taught that businesses are unethical and greedy and that it's only nonprofits that deliver any good in the world. But what we've learned is that when your employees and your customers rally to a common cause, good things—even great things—result. That's because this represents a symbiotic balance, where what we take equals what we get.

The magic happens when you find the sweet spot where your cause, your employees, and your customers intersect. (With or without chips and salsa!) You uncover your company's soul.

The mistake so many organizations make is that they tend to attack each of these different areas as separate "programs." Maybe it's a new customer loyalty campaign you're running, or perhaps it's an employee engagement effort you've recently invested in. It could even be rallying everyone together to do something for a "good cause." But you lose balance when you chase those goals separately.

The magic of the Culture of Good is when you find a way to tackle all those goals **at the same time.** Employees can tell when organizations create efforts like CSR initiatives simply to check a box or salvage their brand. But if you want to reinvent your culture—to embrace the notion of building a Culture of Good—you need to really be authentic and intentional about it.

You can't win someone's heart and mind if you just focus on a new employee engagement program or a new methodology to gain new customers. Both of these miss the "sweet spot"—the soul—where cause, employees, and customers intersect.

For us, it comes back to the message that everyone in our business needs to connect his or her **what** with his or her **why**. When you can do that, you know what you end up with? Happiness. We can admit that slinging cell phones, as the employees at TCC do, is not the most glamorous job in the world. Yes, getting the first crack at playing with the newest toys on the market doesn't exactly suck. But our employees aren't saving lives like ER nurses and paramedics or firefighters and policemen and policewomen do on a daily basis. When you talk to associates at TCC, we think you'll be surprised by how passionate they are about what they do on a daily basis. Why? Because we have collectively learned to appreciate that every time we sell something to a customer, we all have a larger common cause we're working for—and it's not when the transaction ends.

Now imagine what our world would be like if every employee working at a for-profit company went to his or her job every day feeling like he or she was volunteering at a nonprofit organization with a higher purpose? What would happen if we intentionally tore down those walls that separate simply going to work from doing good as a result of our work? There's no better feeling than finding your calling in life and being able to share it with others—to have your **what** equal your **why**. That's the kind of goal we're after by building a Culture of Good. But this outcome doesn't happen by accident. As we've grown the Culture of Good from that initial sketch on a napkin into the core of how we run our business now that it encompasses 800 stores and 3,000 employees, we've had to answer some challenging questions, such as:

- When we're hiring, we want to hire people who will flourish within the Culture of Good. But how do we attract people who will embrace our vision for that?

- How do we, as an organization, teach people (both formally and informally) about how the Culture of Good drives everything we do in our business on a day-to-day basis?

- When someone does something amazing—where he or she is really living out the Culture of Good—what do we do to quickly recognize, celebrate, and reward his or her accomplishments?

- Does our organization encourage people committed to the Culture of Good to stay and thrive? How do we react to employees who don't connect with our norms, values, and beliefs?

- What metrics do we need to track or even create to measure our progress in reaching the goals we have set for ourselves, such as assessing our engagement with the communities we serve?

- When we make a decision, from executive level down to our customer service reps, do we ask how will it impact the lives of our employees, our customers, and our organizational cause?

We also strongly believe that you have to build a financially sustainable business as you start implementing this system. We're not here advocating for some newfangled philanthropy program. Rather, we're experimenting with something new and profound: the idea that **you can do good while you work and that good can drive your bottom line.** As an organization, we rely on systems and processes to keep our stores working smoothly. But every process, every meeting, every checklist needs to tie back to the Culture of Good. It's the *why* behind what we do. Doing good and doing our job don't have to be separated like we've been taught. We all spend so much of our lives working in our jobs. Shouldn't we find just as much fulfillment in that time as we do in our time away from work? When we think about business leaders such as Warren Buffett, Bill Gates, and Mark Zuckerberg pledging their billions to help the world, shouldn't it beg the question about what could have happened if they had been able to do as much good at the time they were building up their businesses? Or, to say that another way, what could the impact have been if they got every one of their employees to join them on that ride all along? Imagine what we can do if we do good *while* we are doing our work in a way that benefits our fellow coworkers, our communities, and our customers. Don't you think that would feed your soul as much as your bank account?

And we totally get the idea that running a business with three dimensions can be hard, especially if you're growing at the rate and to the scale that we are. You almost need to be some kind of Jedi to be able to maintain your focus on doing good as the financial pressures mount during your continued growth. Trying to balance the budget and maintain our fiduciary responsibilities to our employees while also pursuing a purpose as a company is freaking painful.

Real costs ARE associated with running an initiative such as the Culture of Good. And yet the benefits and the payoff from that investment can be intangible and hard to quantify on something like a profit-and-loss statement. Yes, we can talk about how we fed several thousand people by volunteering at a food bank or how in the first year of our School Rocks initiative (more on that later) we helped 60,000 kids by giving them backpacks filled with school supplies. But when you're the CEO who is responsible for bank debt, payroll, and making sure the company continues to operate, the direct connection with investing upward of $400,000 in backpacks or in paying someone's salary for a day as a volunteer may not be obvious. Making decisions like that can give you real headaches. It's hard to sell karma.

But if our company isn't financially sustainable, if it doesn't make enough money to survive, we can kiss the Culture of Good good-bye. That's why it's essential to understand that our culture is not just about plunking down thousands of dollars into a new program and mandating that people take part in it. That won't work. Plenty of companies have tried this approach, including household names, only to see those programs die over time from lack of passion and participation. We've achieved our results by simply shifting our focus on a few budget lines that were there anyway. The financial support to roll out the system came from our ability to upend traditional thinking and reallocate to the progressive mind-set that this would work in the end. It was a bet on the long. The only way it works is by building trust—a ton of it—based on the message that the more people know we do good, the more good we can do. It's about giving your people *permission to care*. That's the purpose we strive for every day, and it's how we feed the soul of our company.

It's a cold, hard fact that if we did away with our Culture of Good efforts at TCC and ran the company along two dimensions, where our goal was to maximize profits at the expense of pursuing a purpose, we might very well make more money. We could then stroke a check and donate a bunch of money to good causes run by other good people. What's wrong with that approach? you might be asking. That's what most companies and successful people do, right? Yes, and taking this approach is neither right nor wrong. A ton of good has been done in the world as a result of donated money.

The challenge we have given ourselves, however, is to put our employees and ourselves out there in a different way. We want to give them permission to care at work. The world already has enough non-profits. That's why our story isn't about how we built some kind of new philanthropic program. Our Culture of Good began as an idea over chips and salsa and sketched out on a napkin. But we also knew that just coming up with a slogan we could slap on the wall wouldn't be enough. We needed the Culture of Good to be woven deeply into the DNA of the organization. It needed to be at the forefront of every interaction with our employees, at every touch point with our customers, and part of every active outreach we made to the communities we operate in. In fact, we've even made this part of how we evaluate every employee, where half of his or her review is based on how he or she impacts the three components of the Culture of Good. Why? Put simply: because we want to make the world a better place and have a shit ton of fun while making a boatload of money. Those are the kinds of impacts and purposes that drive us forward on our journey.

And in case you haven't noticed, today's workers—especially millennials—seek out workplaces that embrace a bigger cause. That means that if you want to attract, or even keep, your best employees, you might need to rethink the connections between doing work and doing good and how they can be directly related. As the famed business guru Peter Drucker said, your best workers have options, and you need to manage them as if they were volunteers. That's why it's essential to create the kinds of conditions that connect the notion of doing good while you do good work for your employees. When you do that, great things can result.

For instance, 92 percent of TCC's workforce is made up of millennials between the ages of 25 and 35. Those younger workers expect a lot from their employer and, as a result, tend to move between jobs quite a bit. In our industry, turnover averages about 66 percent. But the millennials at TCC, especially those between the ages of 25 and 35, tell us that our Culture of Good gives them a sense of fulfillment at work (the average age of our employees is 28.5 for what it's worth). That's a big reason why our turnover is down 25 percent—even though our workforce has more than doubled over the past five years. That's saved the company about $3.7 million a year! People want to work with us because they know they can make a difference in the world where they work.

Since we implemented our Culture of Good at the start of 2013, we've also seen a dramatic impact on the bottom line of our business. Top-line revenues of the business have gone up 200 percent, and same-store sales are up 70 percent; perhaps more impressively, our operating income is up 490 percent. That's right: we're more profitable as a result of embracing the Culture of Good, which has allowed us to do more good as a result. To be more specific, we have multiplied the amount we have donated to good causes by a factor of six since 2012—TCC now contributes $1,300 per employee each year, and rising, to good causes—and that doesn't even count the thousands of hours of volunteer time and personal contributions our employees have made during this period. We've proven that by doing good, you can help grow a profitable company, which then enables you to give back to the world in amazing ways. Outlets such as *People, Forbes, Inc., The Huffington Post*, and *Fox Business* agree. At the time this book went to print, we secured nine national media stories about TCC's Culture of Good, resulting in more than 85 million impressions with an ad equivalency value of $703,954.

Have we blown your mind yet?

But don't just take it from us. Here's what Paul Duyvejonck, one of our regional account managers, wrote us in an e-mail in the wake of our first annual backpack giveaway (which we'll talk about in more detail later):

> *I'm sure you're getting plenty of THANKS from around the team today and will in the near future, but I needed to get this out. I've been involved in many companies "giving back." This usually means giving a donation, or sitting under a tent trying to pretend to be engaged for an hour or so. The fact that you created a culture, and embrace our team relaying this culture throughout the nation, is unspeakable. Like I said, just wanted to give a quick thank you, and I'm anxiously awaiting the next opportunity to truly show why #TCCROCKS.*

Thank you, Paul, for summing up nicely what the Culture of Good is all about—as well as what we mean by finding your company's soul.

Our Journey Continues

It's important to acknowledge that we didn't always know how to reach the goals we set for ourselves. In fact, we're still learning and growing. We weren't following any plan or how-to checklist we had read about (though that might have helped if we had). In truth, we started this journey simply because our hearts told us it was the right thing to do.

Because we were flying by the seat of our pants, letting our hearts tell us what the best path might be, we've made our fair share of mistakes and missteps. The journey started with an idea, and early on, we were just two people with a vision. But over the past few years, as we have shared our vision with the team, we have inspired others to join us on our journey. If you ask people today at TCC about the Culture of Good, you get passionate answers in return. Without much prompting, they will tell you countless stories about how the Culture of Good has made a difference to them, their customers, and the members of the community—which is our shared cause. We've even included some of those stories in the pages that follow.

Maybe we could have had even more of an impact on the lives of our employees, customers, and community members if we had figured out things sooner. What's important is that we have had an impact—a sizable one—in just the few years that we have been on our Culture of Good journey. And our message is starting to spread: we now have other companies approaching us and asking for our help in building their own Culture of Good. We even have had a major children's hospital ask us, a retail company, to come talk to them about what we have been building. A key goal we have is helping you flatten out your own learning curve, which is also the goal behind why we started a new organization called the Culture of Good, whose goal is to help you learn from our own journey of what happens when you give people the permission to care at work.

We both recognize that the experience we went through was something that is very unique to us. But that doesn't mean you can't leverage and build on it. Every one of us has had events in life that have caused us to ask questions such as: Why am I doing what I'm doing? Why am I going to work today? Does what I do in my daily grind really matter?

Maybe it was a personal accident, the loss of a loved one, or even a national tragedy. The list is endless. The point is that in the wake of that moment, did you do anything about it, or did you just go back to your day-to-day?

Our specific set of circumstances gave us the opportunity to create something special. Our call to action was there, and we took it. Perhaps your own call to action will be reading this book. If it is, what kind of action will you be inspired to take next?

In the pages that follow, we'll share what we have done to build our Culture of Good and why. We'll also share the things we tackled that didn't work out. We're continuing to experiment and to push forward as a way to keep our momentum rolling and to avoid what happens to so many cultural nitiatives like this in other companies: apathy. You know, the point where the excitement of something new wears off and everyone just drifts back to doing his or her work the way he or she used to.

That's a real danger, especially if you fail to keep stoking the fires of passion in your people. If done correctly, the power of the Culture of Good is that you achieve long-term sustainability rather than just quick jabs of excitement to the organization. The Culture of Good will keep everyone fired up to come to work and be a part of something bigger from the first day until the last. It becomes a normal daily effort that keeps an elevated sense of worth inside of every one of the company stakeholders. Apathy be damned.

The point is that if you're considering taking your organization down a similar path as we have gone or asking your boss or employer to think about your workplace in a different way, make sure everyone's heart is in the right place first. If you aren't authentic, your employees, your customers, and the members of your community will see right through you and you will fail. If you aren't ready to think beyond the two dimensions of a spreadsheet and believe that you can be even more successful by bringing in that third element of feelings, well, this book probably isn't for you.

We're also challenging you to think about how to tie doing good into the daily routine of how you go about your business. Some organizations do events where, for instance, everyone within the company focuses on community service for one day together. And that's great. Charities such as Habitat for Humanity need help building homes. But your cause (just like your employee and customer engagement efforts) needs to be a year-round focus.

If you are ready to think differently about how you can do good better through your business, to help everyone inside your organization have permission to care on a daily basis, then read on! What follows is a combination of our individual stories and how, beginning at that Mexican restaurant with chips and salsa, we embarked on a journey to try to change the world. Big goals, we know. But that truly is what fuels us. We hope to fuel you as well by sharing our story.

We have written this book together, and so the narrator in the pages that follow reflects that. But we're also very different in how we talk and tell stories, so you'll also see examples of how we write as individuals. We'll start by each sharing our own backstories and the struggles and victories we had in our lives that eventually led us to that chance encounter in church. Then, we'll talk about the early days of the Culture of Good and the different experiments we undertook to lay the foundation for our authentic intentions for what would come later. We'll continue by sharing how we worked to connect magic moments and transform them into a movement. We'll also talk about how we have worked to make the Culture of Good sustainable over the long term rather than having it feel like just another annual program. Next, we'll share recent efforts and some feedback we have received from our employees and partners about the kind of impact the Culture of Good has had on them. Finally, we'll pull it all together and show you the magic of engaging your employees through giving them permission to care. This will empower you to use your COG to show your customers that you have a competitive advantage while driving and leading your business toward greater success.

As a bonus, we've also plugged in a few questions at the end of each chapter for you to reflect and chew on. Asking yourself these questions can also be a way for you to discover your own path to building a Culture of Good. We have shared what finding a company's soul looks like for us; your version will be very different. But our goal is to help you get there.

We hope to inspire you to rethink how your business or the place where you go to work every day can be a force for good in the world and how, by joining together, we can truly change the world. That's what giving people permission to care is all about.

As a way to get started, let us share some more about who we are and where we came from.

Questions to Consider
Scott's questions:

1. Why does your business, or the company you work for, do what it does? What's your higher purpose?

2. Do you think that doing good with your business or your job and making money are complete opposites?

3. Does your organization or the company you work for struggle to maintain millennial workers? Do you want to change that?

Ryan's questions:

1. What kind of good does your organization or the company you work for pursue already? Can you imagine how you could build on that and turn it into a movement?

2. How does your organization engage in a cause that matters? What would it look like if people engaged with your cause actively throughout the year? What difference could you make?

The Backstory 2

If you want to hear the story of how the Culture of Good came to be, you first need to learn about the two main characters who helped drive its creation. That's because we each come from such different places—completely separate ends of the spectrum, really. In one corner was Scott, the academic entrepreneur who was a product of a traditional family upbringing, a college grad, a fast-track executive, and very well-off by the time he was 35. And in the other corner, you had Ryan, who moved 15 times when he was growing up, was educated by doing charity work to better families' lives in America's inner cities, and spent his time raising funds to complete his next big idea to make the world better for the less fortunate.

In each of our minds, we were taking advantage of the other's strengths and what the other person had to offer. As Ryan admits, "I had ideas but limited money, and Scott had money but limited ideas . . . . We needed each other." But, really, our goal was the same: we wanted to give people permission to care at work and in turn make the world better. Our give equaled our take. The magic we created when we teamed up is what makes our journey together worth reading about.

Scott

It was Scott's parents, Steve and Phyllis Moorehead, who taught him about the ingredients that he and Ryan would eventually use to cook up the Culture of Good. But it was up to Scott to discover the full recipe. "They gave me my moral fibers," says Scott. "They were my first mentors, and they taught me the power of giving back. If they had been greedy, none of this would have happened.

"My father followed in his father's footsteps in electrical contracting," says Scott. But Scott's parents later sold that business and started another focused on doing local area networking and business telephone systems. Business telephone systems led them to an opportunity in the world of wireless way back in 1990. They ended up selling the legacy system company and devoting 100 percent of their effort to building a new company in the twilight of their careers. By the mid-1990s, they had grown that business up to 50 locations, all in Indiana.

That was also around the same time that Scott was going to school at Purdue University. He had worked for the local area networking part of the business during the summers. By his second year at Purdue, Scott started working part-time in a TCC retail store right in West Lafayette, Indiana. He continued to work there as a retail sales consultant all the way through school until he graduated.

When he graduated, he started working full-time for his parents. Things were starting to explode within the cell phone industry, and they knew they wanted to eventually transition out of the business. But before they would hand over the reins to Scott, they suggested that he spend time working in every position of the company as a way to really get to know the business inside and out. They wanted to humble him to some degree.

And that's what happened: he spent nine months doing everything from sweeping floors to running payroll and hiring new employees. "It was like I was a powerful young Jedi that they were trying to stop from going to the dark side," says Scott. He learned a lot—especially about his parents' philosophy of treating the people inside the business. His dad had a placard of sorts on his desk all those years that contained the following wisdom: "Hire smart, go bonkers, have grace, make mistakes, love tech, start all

empathy
compassion
fairness
management w/o intimidation
honesty
fair pay
chance for improvement
if people want to come to work

- over 50 years of business if given a multiple choice test most owners would get a 95-100. Very few would pass the "walk"

- the customer is not always right, but the customer is always the customer

A snapshot of Scott's notebook and takeaways from his parents.

over again." Scott even has a picture of a handwritten page of notes he took during a conversation with his parents that included words and phrases such as "empathy," "honesty," "fairness," "management without intimidation," "compassion," "fair pay," and "chance for improvement." He also wrote down that "the customer is not always right, but the customer is always the customer."

Scott's dad was past retirement age and wasn't interested in keeping up with what had become a rapidly growing and dynamic industry. So Scott bought his parents out at a price where he'll still be paying them for years to come! "I took a big chance, and it freaked me out," says Scott, who was just 30 at the time. "But I feel like my parents wouldn't have sold the business to just anyone. They trusted me, which was big."

Scott married his high school sweetheart, Julie, when he turned 25. He then had his first child at 29 and his second (and last) at 31. But the mixture of success at work and the lack of a great work/life balance, combined with some bad lifestyle choices, led to stress in his personal life. Things were starting to fall apart. By the time he turned 35, things were pretty bad personally—and pretty darn good at work. But the stress in his personal life was starting to creep into work efforts and take its toll. The summer of 2012 is not a time that either of us will soon forget. That's the year things got worse, all due to a pure-hearted effort to show his 5-year-old son how to skateboard.

Unfortunately for Scott, he might have lost a few memories from before that time. That's because one day in August of that year he was being a good dad who was spending some time with his son and teaching him how to ride a skateboard. Nothing too crazy—no 360 jumps or half-pipe twists, just skating down the road. But something went wrong, horribly wrong. Scott fell and busted his head open. The result of this was a quadruple contiguous skull fracture, a double hematoma, and, ultimately, a traumatic brain injury.

Fortunately, he was alive. But his brain was damaged, potentially irreversibly. Even as he began his rehabilitation process, it really hit home that something seriously bad had happened when he couldn't complete a simple word search puzzle. "That scared the heck out of me," he says. Even today, he hasn't regained his sense of smell—another consequence of the injury. "It's one of those crazy stories where you realize that life is short and can end in an instant," says Scott. "I was young at the time, and I was successful. So I wasn't thinking about continuity or what would happen in the long run. But then, wham, you get knocked off your pedestal not because you failed but by nearly passing on. It was a 'holy crap' moment for me to realize how everything could get swept away from me so fast."

The good news was that he had already put good people into leadership positions inside the company. That allowed him to recover while knowing that the business could continue until he got back—rather, if he got back.

"That was an interesting transition," says Scott. "Before the accident, I was at the center of so much in the business. And now I was forced to withdraw from that role."

He began to wonder what his future would look like if he didn't get better. How would he provide for his family? Thoughts of working as a greeter at a big retailer haunted his waking moments. He admits that even before the accident, when he was a young and seemingly successful CEO, he had begun to lose sight of what made him happy. He had found success, but it hadn't created happiness. He had begun to lose touch with his soul. The accident only made all the bad parts of his life worse. Scott soon became depressed. He turned to drugs and alcohol as a way to cope. As a result, he started to feel parts of his life spiraling away from him. His life was officially out of control. Both personally and professionally, he was walking a very dangerous line.

Ryan

When Ryan was just 6 years old, his life took a very tragic turn. "I remember coming home from school as I did every day," he says. "But one day everything in my life changed. Within a year of my mom being diagnosed paranoid schizophrenic, her disease caused her to take her own life. I came home from learning to read in the first grade to hearing that my mom was gone. I had to learn to either get bitter toward the world or not pretty quick." Having his mother stolen from him at such a young age wasn't fair. To add to his struggle, his father, a veteran of the Vietnam War, was battling drug addictions.

But Ryan didn't go through this heartbreaking time in his life alone. Along with others, his first-grade teacher, Rebecca Overley, was there for him. "When I went to my mother's funeral, she came for me. When I cried in class, she held me," says Ryan. "Knowing her impact on me during such a difficult time in my young life was undeniable and would ultimately shape my mission in life. When we met again years later, she continued to say, 'Ryan, I was there for you.' The idea of simply being there for people inspired me in my life purpose from that conversation forward. Every one of us has the ability to use our everyday work to be a catalyst for making a positive impact on a person in need." This experience has since become the filter for discovering his life purpose. As Ryan describes it, "I'm still that 6-year-old boy with no mom and a drug-addicted father. This is the whole reason I do what I do. There are other little Ryans out there who need to know someone cares."

When Ryan was 11, he moved to upstate New York, where his family became caretakers at a summer camp. Camp Comanche took disadvantaged kids from the city and brought them up to the Catskill Mountains for the summer. At the young age of 14 he became a camp counselor and began his journey to discover ways he could have a greater impact on others. While Ryan was in New York in the summer of 1993, he also worked for Pastor Bill Wilson, who would become a key mentor of his and from whom he learned a lot about what it means to love and to give back. Pastor Bill always taught Ryan, "The need is the call." "I never forgot that finding my calling meant meeting the needs in the world around me," says Ryan. "That summer in 1993 wrecked my life from being what I would call normal. I had to live for something bigger, something significant."

Years later, with his wife, Katara, Ryan cofounded the Center for Success, an afterschool network for at-risk children. This charitable organization provides youth in need with food, mentors, tutoring services, and athletic programs. The first Center for Success was in his hometown of Marion, Indiana, where he grew up and experienced the loss of his mom. The center has since expanded to Pontiac and Detroit, Michigan, as well as Zambia, Africa, as a school for hundreds of children. "It's rewarding to make a difference in the lives of these deserving children, just as my elementary school teacher did for me in my time of need," says Ryan.

Ryan's father remarried and has been addiction free since 1983. Mrs. Overley, the elementary school teacher who was there for him when he needed someone the most, still keeps in touch to this day. Here's a quote she recently shared with Ryan in a Facebook message:

> *Maybe the journey isn't so much about becoming anything.*
> *Maybe it's about un-becoming everything that isn't really you*
> *so that you can be who you were meant to be in the first*
> *place.*

"If I can offer that understanding to others, then I have accomplished part of my calling in life," says Ryan, who also joined his wife in starting a church in their house, God's House, where Scott and he would eventually make their first connection.

"I remember telling Katara after Scott and I had lunch at that Mexican restaurant about how excited I was for the chance to work with him and to see how I could help plant the seeds of doing good within his company," says Ryan. "He had given me the sense that he wanted to hire me and that it was just a matter of knocking out the paperwork."

Meanwhile, Ryan was admittedly going a bit nuts about what was happening with his potential job at TCC. "It got parked for a while," says Ryan. Then he got a call from Scott's wife, Julie, letting him know that Scott had fallen off a skateboard and was airlifted to emergency care.

Creating the Spark

After Ryan got that call, he began visiting Scott in the hospital while he and Katara and their two girls, Bria and Brenna, also spent time with Julie and their kids, Mason and Marlee. "I remember having a couple of conversations with Scott as he suffered from really severe headaches," Ryan recalls. "During one of those talks, he told me about how he had come to newly appreciate the need for a family and friends and being loved. He said that was the stuff in life that mattered most. But he also talked about leaving a greater legacy with his company, that he wanted to pursue the things we had talked about back at that Mexican restaurant."

"I had a shift in my life," says Scott, who also admits he doesn't completely remember those bedside talks. "My focus switched from the success of the company to the legacy that I could leave. It became important to me to make an impact. And the assets I had to do that were my organization."

Eventually, as Scott slowly got better and ultimately left the hospital, he made the decision to bring Ryan on full-time in February 2013—the exact same day that he also hired Katie Wiley, his in-house attorney.

"I was convinced that he would eventually hire me," says Ryan.

"I don't have the same amount of certainty that Ryan does that he was going to come work for us," says Scott. "I wasn't sure what he would do."

"I didn't either," says Ryan with a laugh.

"When I hired Ryan and Katie, my brain wasn't functioning at a particularly high level," says Scott.

"Which worked out for us because I might not have been hired if your brain was working," says Ryan.

"Ha, read into it what you want," says Scott. "But the idea of building a legacy has definitely become a priority for me. I wanted to add folks like you and Katie, who could help me with that effort."

By January of 2014, Scott's life hit bottom. After being tossed out of his own house and family, he was faced with a choice: get help or keep going down the same path where he'd probably end up divorced and, eventually, dead. He decided to pull himself out of work and get help. He then spent three months in rehab, where he spent countless sessions with psychologists, counselors, and coaches.

One huge lesson that Scott came to realize and that he now teaches is that he needed to be happy, first, before he could become successful. With an unrelenting will to save his family and his life, Scott stayed close to Ryan. And even as they worked on the Culture of Good together, Scott believes Ryan was secretly working on him as well. With that help, Scott evolved over time into what his friends now call Scott 2.0. "Hitting bottom as Scott 1.0 and having the timing work out the way it did gave way to what was a relentless focus on figuring out how to show everyone in the path ahead that happiness came first and success would follow," says Scott. "This gave jet fuel to the effort and determination to achieve a Culture of Good."

Now that Scott was back, he needed Ryan's help with finding ways for his company to transform as well. All the ingredients were in place. They just needed to find the right recipe to bring them together to evolve from a Culture of OK into a Culture of Good.

The question was, what did the first step in that journey look like?

Questions to Consider
Scott's questions:

1. Where do you find your happiness?

2. What do you want people to take away with them when they hear your story?

3. If you are a leader of your organization, have you surrounded yourself with clones or with people who are different from you?

Ryan's questions:

1. In what ways can you live bigger in your world more than what your title or role dictates?

2. What are you doing now to affect what people would say about you at your funeral? How do you want to be remembered?

3. How can you take the pain of your past and use it as a way to discover your calling and purpose?

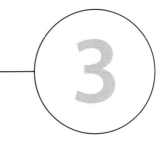

Authenticity and Intention

As we began our journey together to build a Culture of Good, remember that TCC already had a strong and established culture in place—even if we didn't know what to call it—long before Scott made the decision to bring Ryan on board. The company was already doing plenty of good; it's just that no one knew it!

Far from being a start-up, the company had been growing like gang-busters and had attracted and retained a strong group of employees who supported that growth. In those days, the company, which everyone called Moorehead, was known for its freewheeling and willingness to chase every big opportunity that came along. Without knowing any better, we tack-led huge programs with national retailers and celebrities without any real thought about whether we could actually pull them off. But that was part of the spirit of the business at the time. It wasn't unlike what you might see at a Silicon Valley start-up, where young, talented, and ambitious people are drawn together to change the world. At that time, everyone knew just about everyone else inside the company. And we were willing to invest in building relationships with our partners to keep our growth on the fast track: anyone could join a dinner or bar outing just about any day of the week. Alcohol was a constant presence in meetings inside the office and out: we recently estimated that we were expensing something like $70,000 a month in booze!

It was a fun place to work. But it was also chaotic. We saw opportunities behind every corner, and we tried to chase down every one, which created more than a few disconnects. When we asked some of our long-term employees to look back on those days, they used words such as "experimental," "immature," and "hyper." People began to see us take a wait-and-see approach to any new program that might emanate from the corporate offices because everything had a kind of "flavor-of-the-month" feel to it. No one was confident about what would stick and what wouldn't. "Our immaturity and lack of visibility and communication were causing all kinds of problems," says Scott. "We were trying to salvage what we could to make sure everyone could be taken care of. We were trying to grow the company to save it. But it felt like chaos and that there weren't any rules in place."

At the same time, people also felt like they were part of something special, a family unit of sorts that was on a mission. While the best people had plenty of opportunities to leave for other jobs, they stayed for that camaraderie as well as the sense that if they did leave, they would miss out on something special. We all just had that feeling that TCC was on the cusp of that something special.

Growth also brought the threat of change, which was especially troubling to Scott. While he thoroughly enjoyed the free-spirited nature of the company he was building, he also worried that as the company continued to grow, it would lose the seeds at the heart of the culture that made it such a special place to work. And he knew things were only going to get worse. He knew that if the business was to survive in a cutthroat industry, it would need to get even bigger. But the faster the company grew, the bigger the threat would become that the glue that held everyone together would melt away. Was there a trade-off between building a big company and building a company that still had that feel of working as a family? For example, for years, Scott's parents had pledged to the company that they would never be open on Sundays. That had to change if TCC was going to become one of the premier wireless dealerships in the country. But when that change was made, many employees didn't understand why it was made, and many just assumed it was because Scott was greedy and uncaring. "Many people started to blame the 'dreaded they' for these kinds of changes that were happening," says Scott. "As in, 'they' decided to do something—meaning me or someone who worked in the corporate offices. The people in the field were starting to feel like they weren't being heard." He is also the first one to admit that he did a piss-poor job at communicating with everyone about why changes like that were taking place. But how could he remedy that?

That was precisely the question that was on his mind when he heard Ryan's sermon about connecting your *why* to your *what*. If they needed TCC to keep growing, he had to find a way to let everyone know why that was so crucial. Hiring Ryan to stoke the fires of the Culture of Good was a step in that direction.

Joining Forces

After he hired Ryan, Scott sent the following e-mail to the whole company:

> *When I sent out my e-mail to introduce our new director of employee and customer relations, Ryan McCarty, I was so excited for you to see what was coming in the next few months. Well, a few months are now past, and we have a great plan to start to show you when we show up to work at TCC that our WHY EQUALS OUR WHAT!! Ryan is*

31

ready to introduce you to a new facet of our culture that will have a great deal of impact on our business, employees, and customers. This new movement has my direct endorsement and is at the top of my priority list to make this one stick. This company will take its blessings and use it to do good for this world. The impact that we make on people who need it can last a lifetime. The effect it can make on our business will be positive. And the PASSION that we have for WHY we do WHAT we do will be the fuel. Please choose to take this opportunity to follow my lead and do this together as we set out to create our Culture of Good.

He closed the e-mail by quoting the lead singer from the band Phish: "Throw away stuff you don't need in the end, keep what's important, and know who's your friend" —Trey Anastasio.

Of course, not everyone inside the company knew what to make of the newest coworker. Ryan's first days on the job coincided with Katie Wiley's, the new attorney. While everyone had a sense of why Katie was brought on board (though many wondered whether Scott or someone else had screwed something up), many still had plenty of questions about why a pastor—especially one who sported a Mohawk at the time—had joined the team. There were more than a few whispers that maybe Scott hadn't fully recovered from his injury or rebounded from his depression.

The truth was that getting back to work was an arduous process for Scott. He was relearning not only how to use his brain but also how to manage and run his business—to become more of a leader than a micromanager. He admits he wasn't always so successful at it, especially in the first year or so he was back at work. "Reintegrating myself was very difficult," says Scott. "But I was also energized with the idea of empowering other people to do their jobs. Getting myself out of the way became crucial if we were going to succeed."

That included giving Ryan the leeway to be creative in his own way in building the foundation for the Culture of Good. "When I came into the company, it was like an explosion of opportunity for me," says Ryan. "I had all kinds of ideas, and I love the space for creativity that Scott gave me. It was also a new concept coming from the nonprofit world that if I came up with an idea, we could actually pay to make it happen!" What Ryan was immediately drawn to was the idea that he could help connect the folks at TCC with a cause bigger than themselves. What he knew how to do well was connect people with the communities they lived and worked in. To put that another way, Ryan helped put us on a path where our cause became making communities better. And his first step was to build a connection to that cause with our employees. That was what we started calling "the Culture of Good."

In his introductory e-mail to the company, Ryan wrote the following:

> *I'm excited to launch our Culture of Good with all of you here at TCC. Each of us plays an important role in making a difference through our TCC community. As we embark on this movement toward leveraging our influence and resources, my hope is that our passion as a company will show our customers and communities that we truly do care. There are so many needs present in our world, and the greatest thing we can do is to do all we can to meet those needs. Doing good every day through TCC will keep WHAT we do in business being driven by WHY we are in business. Our why is the difference we can make together. In the coming days you can expect to get more of the nuts and bolts of this movement to explain how it all works in what is called the Culture of Good Tour Guide. Let's keep doing good together!*

What Ryan didn't know (at least until we started writing this book) was that Scott's decision to bring him on was met with some guarded skepticism, maybe even some cynicism, from other leaders in the company who wondered why in the heck a pastor was getting hired.

"I live under the assumption that everyone loves and appreciates me," says Ryan sarcastically. "I also assumed that everyone in the company had this general appreciation for what we were trying to do. Of course, I couldn't tell right away who was hesitant about the idea or who disagreed with it. But it was an interesting time to step into the company because people were so busy working on other things."

Ryan was shielded by some of the skepticism because he reported directly to Scott, who realized that it was imperative that Ryan work for him one-on-one, at least in the beginning. "I think if he had reported to someone else on my staff, he would have run into a lot more resistance," says Scott, who tasked Ryan early on with putting together some "decks" of initiatives that could be the foundation for the cause component of our Culture of Good.

But the term "deck," which is something lots of corporate execs know lots about, wasn't something Ryan had ever heard before, so he did his best to come up with a proposal using an old-fashioned Microsoft Word document.

Here is an original memo Ryan sent to Scott in early 2013. What's amazing is to look back and see that we did all of this—and much more.

A Culture of Good
Three Areas of Philanthropy

1. #TCCRocks Day:
Stores receive up to $500 total per year to be used toward community volunteer events. After managers pick the event and submit the "Day of Doing Good" form to their regional VP for approval, the manager will coordinate with employees encouraging store involvement. Store employees will volunteer two or more hours depending on event selected. VPs will be encouraged to attend events when available to build interest in doing good. Employees will take pics during event with Instagram #[Store location] and #TCCRocks. VPs can encourage combining stores' efforts to strengthen involvement and finances.

- Manager selects volunteer event and submits Day of Doing Good form to VPs.
- TCC sends up to $500 toward requested support for event to store.
- Manager coordinates store involvement.
- Store volunteers two or more hours depending on event.
- Everyone takes pics with Instagram and #[Store location] and #TCCRocks.
- VPs can select and combine efforts for personal involvement.

2. Two days off per year to volunteer:
Employees receive normal compensation and an additional $25 bonus toward any in-store purchase for each eight-hour day of service.

continues ▷

Employees must complete and submit the Day of Doing Good form to be approved by their local manager 1 month prior to taking the day off. Only one employee per store may take off on any given day after completing three months of employment following hiring. Employees will take pics during the day with Instagram and #[Store location] and #TCCRocks.

- Employee submits Day of Doing Good form to local manager.
- Employee takes pics with Instagram and #[Store location] and #TCCRocks.

3. Round Up
At POS, each customer can opt to round up his or her purchase to the dollar, in turn donating the change to assist TCC's local backpack giveaway for area school children.

- Employee encourages customer to round purchase to nearest dollar.
- Backpacks will be given away at stores to local school children in August.
- Employees take pics with Instagram and #[Store location] and #TCCRocks.

Ryan began doing what he knew to do by having limited help in his other organizations. He put a template together for a website, designed T-shirts, mapped out social media programs, and began to lay out a plan for communicating to the rest of the company what this Culture of Good thing was really all about. "I had zero idea of what I was getting into," Ryan admits. "My hair was on fire, and I was running around in circles with a smile on my face."

"We basically tried any crazy idea Ryan came up with," says Scott. "Not all of them, but most. Ryan was quite independent and did a lot of barreling through on his own. I didn't hit the brakes much on him. The way we worked together was that I could help refine the idea, usually by scaling it up and making it even bigger and crazier as a way to ensure we got the message out to thousands of people in hundreds of remote locations."

Looking back, it's easy to see that we were successful in those early days because of the brute force of our partnership and how we harnessed chaos into something good. Also helpful was that we didn't work within the constraints of a typical corporation that would enforce a lot of structure and rigor over return on investment. But we recognized that a lot of the positive returns, especially in the earliest days, were invisible. You could see them but not touch or measure them. That's not something a typical manager or CEO would stick his or her neck out for. You lose your job that way—maybe even end your career.

Not that any of it was easy for us; it was hard as heck, especially as the organization continued to get bigger and suffered growing pains all at once. Ryan in particular struggled with the notion of how he could knock down those communication barriers that stood between the Culture of Good and the rest of the company.

"I tend to be the kind of person who stays up all night for a week straight knocking things out. In the early years of nonprofit work, my wife and I weren't used to depending on other people to get things done. I didn't know the kind of support I would need to pull off any of the things I had sent to Scott. I had ideas about initiatives we could do but very little understanding of how we could execute on them."

"Ryan is like a race horse," says Scott. "You point him in the right direction and let him go. He knew how to get stuff done, just not inside a big company. My role was to talk things out with him and help him maneuver. I never had to suggest massive changes; it was just giving him confidence while also showing him how he needed to document things as procedures and guidelines. I played a buffer for him early on, but it didn't last. Eventually he figured it all out."

And the first big step Ryan had to learn to take was how to get the word out to the rest of the company and get them on board with the Culture of Good.

The Fortune Cookies

Dateline: April 2013. The challenge: how do we start connecting our employees, our customers, and members of our cause, our community, to our Culture of Good? Now that Ryan was on board full-time, we needed to find a way to begin to get the word out that when you either worked for TCC or bought something from us, you were also giving back to your community. But how?

The answer we arrived at was fortune cookies. A ton of them—500,000 of them, in fact. Price tag: $37,150. We know; it seems kind of crazy now, especially since some of our stores are still finding unopened boxes of the things going on four years afterward. But we had a method to our madness.

We wanted to give something to every customer who walked into our stores to help make the connection with the Culture of Good, which we sometimes used interchangeably with our Twitter handle, #TCCRocks. We wanted to come up with something that would be fun for the customers and employees. "I seem to remember one of our first ideas was giving away water bottles," says Ryan. "But those are expensive. So after doing some online searching for interesting ways to create customized messaging, I eventually hit on the idea of custom-made fortune cookies. I mean, who doesn't love a fortune cookie?"

That said, when Ryan brought the idea to Scott, he was surprised how quickly he jumped on board. In fact, his original proposal was to order something like 50,000 cookies. But, as is his habit, Scott immediately upped the ante by making it bigger and suggesting that they order 500,000 instead.

"We wanted to create a great customer service experience, something that had that old-fashioned white glove kind of feel," says Scott, who can now admit they perhaps overshot on that initial order. "But we also wanted it to be cheeky and fun. I have followed my wife into plenty of stores that hand you a glass of champagne as part of your retail experience. We weren't going to do that. But we wanted something between a top-end Ritz Carlton experience and what you would find at a Shoe Carnival, which is a shoe store with an atmosphere like a circus. It was a great place to bring kids, but maybe it could also drive you nuts. We wanted to find someplace in the middle, where those two ideals overlapped, where we could give our customers something they couldn't get anyplace else. And that's when Ryan came up with this idea of creating our own messages printed inside fortune cookies that could be handed out inside the stores."

For context, it helps to know that we had recently just begun another #TCCRocks initiative we called Round Up that basically was a way for the folks in our retail shops to ask customers whether they would be willing to round up their bill and donate the difference to a good cause; this would become our backpack giveaway, which we'll soon talk about in more detail.

But we also wanted a way to further connect our customers with the good that we were doing at that point and into the future, which is what sparked the idea for giving them a fortune cookie inside the bag with their new purchase.

Let's pause for a second. You're curious about what kinds of messages we had printed up in all those cookies, aren't you? Well, we had five different messages:

1. "You are part of the Culture of Good when you shop TCC."

2. "By rounding up your last dollar, you can become a difference maker with TCC. See #TCCRocks online to see the difference."

3. "Good things happen to you when you do good for others."

4. "You will be happier by giving to others versus giving to yourself. #TCCRocks"

5. "You can give hope to others by volunteering in your community. Search #TCCRocks to see the difference you are making."

Genius, right? Well, we thought so. And so when Ryan drove a truck down to Indianapolis in July 2013 to pick up the delivery and bring it back to our own warehouse, where we could then ship the cookies out again to each of our stores, we were pumped. We couldn't wait to see what everyone thought and how our message would soon go viral.

A pre-bearded Ryan basks in the glow of his batch of golden cookies.

We waited. And waited. And waited some more until we recognized that everyone inside the company wasn't as excited as we were by the idea of handing out fortune cookies. Katie Wiley, our in-house attorney, told Scott: "Great, now we're giving out food. What's next, turkeys?" There was similar confusion about the cookies out in the field. While some stores were enthusiastic about handing out cookies to customers, others ate theirs instead. Worse, one of our store managers in the Boston area even admitted that aside from supplementing their lunches with plenty of free cookies, his store actually started using some as packing peanuts for when they shipped out products to other stores!

Our fortune cookie experience illustrates why so many well-intentioned initiatives die within companies. You could say we even came up with the perfect example of a "flavor-of-the-month" program (insert drum roll). We learned that you can't change an organization's culture with a single good intention.

With the benefit of hindsight, Ryan says it would have been more effective if he had gone to the different department heads in the company and got them on board with the initiative and what its purpose was.

"We were still trying to identify as a company the best way to communicate our message out to all the stores," says Ryan. "I was still brand new and cutting my teeth. The only way I knew how to start was by sending everyone e-mails and hoping they would open them. But I'm not sure most people knew why these boxes of cookies were showing up and what they were supposed to do with them. Sure, some stores gave them away. But I'm not sure they knew why they were giving them out."

We've actually come to think of the fortune cookies as a kind of inside joke, an early failure and learning experience. But now that we look back, we're not so sure it wasn't really a success. It got people talking. Just as importantly, it got us closer to hitting the sweet spot at the center of cause, employees, and customers: the Culture of Good.

Our goal wasn't to go out and tell our customers: "Hey, we're already doing an intense amount of good, so give us money!" Rather, we were trying to get the word out in a grassroots kind of way and get our salespeople to spark conversations with their customers about the kinds of initiatives we were running and how, by spending money with us, they were also giving back to their community.

The barrier we ran into was that our people didn't yet believe that the Culture of Good was an authentic message. So they weren't totally buying it. Maybe it was a new sales gimmick. Or maybe it was just another temporary program that would soon go away. We can't blame them for thinking that. That's when we learned that we needed more than a single intention.

Those fortune cookies got the ball rolling, even if just slowly at first. They began to make those connections, and once people began to become vocal in support of the Culture of Good, things started to click. "What we wanted to do was help confirm that we were hardwiring this great culture of ours into our company and stapling it deep inside us," says Scott. "We wanted to help everyone understand that even as we continued to grow, the part of the company that felt like a family wasn't going away." And when we look back at that money we spent, it begins to look like a great investment. Think about it as if it were a marketing campaign. We got 500,000 impressions for that $37,000, which amounts to just over 7 cents apiece. That's a pretty phenomenal return compared to, say, what you get from running a paid search campaign.

What we learned is that it doesn't really cost much to win the hearts and minds of your people. That notion was implanted even deeper a few months later when we had the first really big win in our Culture of Good efforts: our first backpack giveaway.

Questions to Consider

Scott's questions:

1. Do you feel like your company has a cause? How do you define it?

2. Do you feel like that cause fits with your culture, or does it fight it?

3. Have you ever been part of something at your company that wasn't authentic or genuine? If so, how did that turn out?

Ryan's questions:

1. Does your company's cause connect with your personal values?

2. If you were to use two or three words to define what your current organizational culture looks and feels like, what would you say?

3. Now ask your key people or peers the same question. How do their answers differ from yours?

Connecting Moments into a Movement

Even as we began to build momentum for our Culture of Good, we knew we would still face difficulties in getting people to buy into the *why* behind the *what* of our actions. We needed to do a better job at connecting everyone with the vision of where we wanted to go. Our experience with the fortune cookies taught us that we needed to find ways to hit that sweet spot—to find a cause that our employees and our customers could truly believe in and rally around. It was our chance to pounce and rock it out.

The irony was that the company was already doing plenty of good through the donations made by the Moorehead Family Foundation, which used a percentage of TCC's profits to help support nonprofits in the Indianapolis area. That was a tradition started by Scott's parents, who cut a big check every year to local charities on behalf of the company. But we had also carried on the tradition of doing such a poor job of communicating this to employees that most didn't even know we were doing any of this good. How, then, could we remedy this and get everyone on the same page of feeling good about the cause we were pursuing as an organization to do good in the communities where we operated? We needed some kind of moment, an event of some kind to energize everyone about our collective potential. We needed something that was simple and standardized enough that we could get all of our stores engaged with it.

The answer we arrived at was backpacks.

Just as he had helped us connect our cause with giving back to communities, Ryan led the way by leaning back on what he had learned from his prior work. He had been doing backpack giveaways, where kids would get a new backpack filled with school supplies, for almost a decade through his church. "We wanted to find a way to meet a tangible need in our community," says Ryan. "I had heard about the idea of giving away backpacks as a way to help families and kids who couldn't afford to get new supplies for the school year."

Consider that the average parent with a child in grade school spends about $95 on school supplies such as notebooks, pencils, and a backpack. But for many families, spending that kind of money, especially on more than one child, is financially impossible. That money needs to go toward other expenses, such as food, housing, and utility bills.

The trouble is that without those supplies, or even the sense of pride and self-esteem that can result from showing up for a new school year prepared to tackle some classwork, those same kids can fall further and further behind. That's where the backpacks come into play: they're a way to give those kids and families a reason to smile.

When Ryan was giving backpacks away through his church, he started with a couple dozen. The next year, he gave away 150 backpacks. Then, he gave away 250 the next year. Eventually, 1,000 kids lined up outside the church to wait with their families to get their head start on the new school year.

So when Scott asked for ideas about what TCC could do to make an impact, a backpack giveaway immediately came to mind for Ryan. "I thought we could scale it up and give away 25,000 of them," says Ryan about his initial pitch to Scott.

"My first question to him was, 'How much is this going to cost?'" says Scott. "But I wasn't focused on that as much as I didn't think it was big enough."

Scott started doing some math. If they gave away 25,000 backpacks in the 300 stores operating at that time, that was, like, 83 a store. That wasn't big enough—even if each backpack and set of supplies cost about $8. "I said, 'Let's give away 60,000 of them, 200 a store,'" says Scott, noting that the final tab came to an impressive $417,597. "I had already cut a check for $37,000 for fortune cookies, so this was an easy call." The call was made even easier when Scott recognized that the dollars could come from reallocating money that was already in the marketing budget. In other words, doing all that good wasn't going to cost the company or its employees an extra dime. "It didn't seem like a big risk, and it was easy to see how it had a triple purpose of being good for the business, the employees, and the kids," says Scott. "I said, 'What the hell; why not do this?'"

The backpacks were also potentially a great way to promote the Culture of Good both internally within the company and externally in the communities where the stores operated. "I was so thankful to Scott for believing in my crazy idea," says Ryan. "I mean, who is willing to invest that much money into an idea like that? It says a lot about his leadership and passion. And it meant so much to have that kind of support coming into the company. Every day I wake up, I am so grateful."

Yet not everyone saw it the same way that we did. Some folks inside the company saw the giveaway as a great promotional campaign, a chance to stick a coupon inside each pack as well as a way to bring those families back and turn them into customers.

This is where Ryan put his figurative foot down in a big way. "We needed this to be truly authentic and to prove to our employees that this wasn't some kind of gimmick. If we had let this slide, it would have left a bad taste in everyone's mouth. I didn't want to lose the why behind what we were doing."

At the same time, Ryan would be the first one to admit that since this was his first major rodeo in terms of orchestrating a giveback initiative inside the company, he didn't exactly know how to pull it all together.

Creating a Special Moment

A great example of that subtle inexperience was not really thinking ahead to how you exactly deal with 60,000 backpacks when they arrive. Where the heck do you put them? "We really weren't prepared for them," says Ryan. Worse, we also had to find a way to then ship all of them back out the door again to each of the stores. It was a logistical nightmare.

The good news was that when the first semis started rolling up with the seemingly endless number of shrink-wrapped palettes containing the backpacks, Ryan was able to get the warehouse workers, without any prior notice, to jump on their forklifts and clear out space in an unused portion

of the company's warehouse to store them in. "I never heard one complaint," says Ryan. "I think they actually enjoyed it. It was something that brought everyone together. On that day, the guy running the forklift was as important as our CEO."

In the end, it took plenty of effort to first receive and then ship out those backpacks. "We made it happen," says Ryan.

The question remained, however, about whether anyone was actually going to show up and collect those backpacks. We had been running our Round Up initiative over the prior months, where we asked customers to round up their purchase and donate the difference toward buying backpacks, but we weren't sure how that message was coming across. We also didn't allocate any marketing to the giveaway and left any PR efforts up to the local stores. We treated it like a grassroots effort.

Here is a sample of the kind of e-mail Ryan, who took to calling himself the "Rock Star of Good," was sending out to the company to get everyone prepared for the big backpack giveaway day:

Here are the standings for the top 10 stores that have raised the most monies to date through Round Up and local donations. Please send out to your stores but keep reminding that it's not about the money—it's about the message. The more our customers give, the more they have joined us in making good happen for kids in our communities. Keep up the good work. There are some stores I have spoken with that I feel haven't completely understood this good we are attempting to do. If there is any way I can assist in spreading this Culture of Good movement in your area, please let me know. Each store should know that the "School Rocks Backpack Giveaway" is happening on Saturday, August 3rd, from 12 to 2 p.m. Here are a few other things every store needs to know ...

1. *July is the month of BUZZ. Each store should be calling their local United Way to ask them to help spread the word about our backpack giveaway. (Other BUZZWORTHY ideas: hand out flyers, call local police and fire chief, call YMCA, call Boys and Girls Club, call local library, call local media outlets: newspaper, radio, TV stations).*
2. *They should have all the backpacks already delivered to their store. If not, please let me know, as there have been a few stores that I heard have not received them yet. This is very important!*
3. *There will likely be a second shipment to many of the larger-market stores in a couple of weeks if we have additional backpacks that have not been allotted. If any store would like to request more, they can do so by simply e-mailing me the number and I will do my best to supply them.*

4. *They should have received 2 marketing pieces. One is a table tent to position on the POS counter. The other is a wall backpack display. The wall display has a calculator that they can print a basic label depicting their total amount of monies raised from their customers' Round Up. This can be displayed behind the POS station.*

5. *I will be sending out a "School Rocks Backpack Giveaway Event" e-mail in a couple weeks describing how we are all going to make the day of event happen together at each store. Watch for it and update your team when it goes out.*

Again, I can't emphasize enough how each of our stores needs to have leadership that have committed to our Culture of Good. You are that leader. I need each of you to believe that when we do good, we are truly living the WHY in all the WHAT that we do every day. Thank you for being a huge part of our TCC family becoming known for the good we do for kids in our community. If I can help in any way or answer any questions you may have, let me know.

The truth was we had no idea whether any of this was going to work. "I was scared that no one would show up," says Ryan. Scott was, too. While he had done his best to send word out to all of the stores in the field, it was going to be up to them whether people knew when and where to show up.

Giveaway Day

As the days on the calendar ticked off until the big event, which was held on a Saturday, a few good signs emerged that the word was getting out about the backpack giveaway. "I remember driving out to visit one store, and the manager was acting like this was going to be the biggest event in the world," says Ryan. "He started calling me three times a day in the week leading up to it. He had hired cheerleaders and called the police and fire department to let them know as a way to spread the word. He even had a pizzeria donate food for the event."

But when the big day came, Ryan couldn't shake a sense that something was wrong. "I remember being on the phone with Katara and telling her that it felt like I had a dark cloud hanging over my head. I was just hoping it wasn't going to suck too much. I was hoping to god someone showed up."

The problem was that no one had ever tried to do anything like this, at this scale. We're sure someone probably had, but we didn't know about it, and we certainly didn't have any blueprint for how to draw it up. We were winging it for the most part and put some serious money into something whose outcome was unknown.

As he continued to drive and get closer to the store in West Lafayette, Indiana, Ryan heard something strange on the radio. It was a live feed coming from the store. The local radio station had set up a mobile booth and was broadcasting and letting people know to come on down and join the fun—and join the fun they did, as 1,000 people were lined up by the time Ryan rolled in. "When I heard and saw that, I begin to think this was really going to work," says Ryan. "I was so excited because it had never even occurred to me that there would be enough people showing up that they would have to get into lines."

For his part, Scott was staked out at his wife's parent's house, where he followed all the updates via his phone. A nonstop text thread had begun where people from all the different stores were sharing updates and photos from across the country. Scott was particularly interested in an update he received from Talitha Troupe, an employee who works in a TCC store in Pennsylvania. She had mentioned to Scott beforehand how she had made a very personal promise to one certain girl in the Marion area that she would get one of the first backpacks.

Talitha Troupe and her young friend embrace.

When Scott later saw a picture of Talitha and the girl embracing and crying, the new backpack on the shoulders of the young girl, he knew that no matter what else happened, that day was now a success. That was a special moment. "I knew we had done everything for the right reasons," says

Scott, who, after wiping his own eyes, then forwarded that picture to his entire executive team. "It was worth every penny we had spent to create a moment like that. It just felt right. It was at that moment that the Culture of Good captured 150 percent of my heart. It was then that it became part of my DNA."

Indeed, that first backpack giveaway was a great success. The day saw much more hugging, dancing, and, yes, tears of joy. Not only did 60,000 kids get to start their school year off with the tools they needed to succeed but also our company had laid the foundation for all of our employees to recognize how we could do good better. We had learned how to engage other people in the community, including firefighters, police, and the media, and join with us in doing good and helping kids in their community. And the results were amazing.

For days and weeks after, Scott and Ryan received e-mails from employees sharing their experiences, with many calling that day the best moment of their entire *career*. Talk to just about anyone at TCC and he or she will have a moment from a backpack giveaway day where his or her heart melted as well—from the young girl who needed extra time to pick the color she wanted to the hug they received from a parent who was sobbing out of gratitude. Then there was the young boy who on receiving the last backpack at a store looked behind him and, seeing a young girl standing next in line, handed it to her instead. Generosity really is contagious (and we made sure we got that boy a backpack of his own as well). Sharing those moments with each other and with you has real power.

What made the difference between the backpacks and the fortune cookies was that rather than giving away something that was fun, we were giving away something that someone genuinely appreciated. That gave everyone a true feeling of elation. "Our people immediately felt a sense of purpose and meaning in their job that might not have been there before," says Scott. "When a CEO writes a check for a charity, he or she gets to bask in the adulation of giving away a bunch of money. But the employees don't feel like it's their work." At the same time, if a business creates activities for its employees that don't enable them to actually connect with the folks connected to the organization's cause, then it comes across as too narcissistic, like, "Look at the good stuff we are doing!" But when the organization says to someone involved in a cause, "Hey, there's this issue over here. We think we can all pitch in and make a difference. Here's what we're doing. We'd love your help," then a shift occurs: you're not an organization selling to a cause; you're an organization engaging with a cause.

That backpack giveaway day gave everyone inside the company the feeling that the company cared about more than just our shared cause—our community—we also cared about them, in giving them the chance to participate in such a momentous day. You can't do that with fortune cookies alone.

What that day taught us was that beyond our ability to give a lot of stuff away, which we had proven we could do, we had found a way to grab the hearts of our employees. We had found a way to show them why we do what we do. It's not a reach to think that the giveaway day brought the company together in a way that no other thing could have done.

That was crucial because not every store participated as much as others. Maybe we didn't get through to them via the e-mail or they didn't yet understand what we were striving for. But when they saw the e-mails and the pictures, we got even more e-mails and requests for information on what we were going to do next year. "That's when even we were like, 'Holy crap, this works!'" says Scott. "We now have an opportunity to drive participation throughout the company because everyone gets it. We're no longer selling an idea. The dream has become reality. It was time to pounce on that and begin to build it from there."

Certainly, the backpack giveaway has only gained momentum from that first year; it's gotten bigger every year. In 2016, TCC gave away

135,000 backpacks. Even better, we helped inspire one of our partners in the telecom business to give away an additional 100,000, for a total of 235,000 backpacks to kids in need. Think about the impact that has! It's no surprise, therefore, that so many TCC employees think of the backpack giveaway day as a kind of holiday, something they look forward to all year. For some, their biggest regret is the fact that they weren't able to give more time to the giveaways we held the first few years. In fact, it's become something of a family affair, where many employees now bring their kids with them to participate. "That day has become a way for all of us to set an example for our kids that our job doesn't have to be a place that sucks," says Scott. "So many kids have the experience where their parents are stressed out and angry by the time they come home at the end of the day. And you know the kids are like, 'What happens at that place mom and dad call "work"?' But when you can bring your kids to your job and it's a place where people are smiling and having fun, wow, what a cool thing."

In other words, we were ready to take the positive energy we had built by creating that moment and turn it into a cadence of many moments that would encompass a movement.

Hitting the Sweet Spot

As an organization, we started by distributing fortune cookies, only to watch them take on a second, unintended, life as packing peanuts. Now, we had learned how to engage communities by distributing backpacks. We have talked a lot about our efforts to establish a Culture of Good in our company. But it's important to recognize that this is a vehicle to get us to our ultimate goal, which is the sweet spot at the center of the Culture of Good. That remains at the core of what we continue to build, and it all dates back to that first lunch we had at the Mexican restaurant. It was there that Scott mapped out the three components of what we initially called the virtuous circle of success on a napkin. The idea was that each

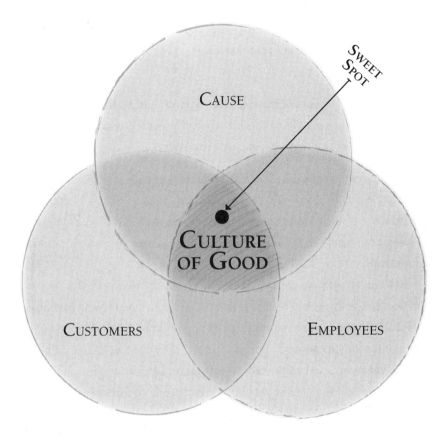

of these elements—employees, customers, and cause—must be in balance with each other for the culture to be sustainable.

While these definitions have continued to evolve, especially regarding how we connect and engage our customers with our cause, this is what we wrote at the time to help describe what the elements of the Culture of Good meant to us and our company:

- When community matters—we support the people in the communities where our stores are located by giving of our time and money.

- When customers matter—we provide them with outstanding service and sincere care that meets their unique needs at a competitive price.

- When employees matter—we create a culture that inspires and motivates people to reach their full potential while also being a part of the company's greater purpose.

If any one component has less focus and energy invested in it, the company loses its "Way of Life," or sense of balance, which is the basis for beliefs and purpose to passionately pursue the realization of making a difference equally in the lives of our employees, our customers, and the communities where we live.

"When we are passionate about making a difference in the lives of the people our company touches, we will succeed," says Ryan. Passion is intrinsic and must be recognizable in each employee. Intrinsic motivators drive our company toward success. Success is defined by being empowered to do more good resourced by our financial attainments. Success is also defined by the good we inspire others outside of our company to do because our passion sparks good in them. Success happens by more than simply making money or just doing good. Only when we seek to make more money and in turn do more good have we realized success. The why of financial attainment is the motivator to what we attain financially. Our *why* should equal our *what*; our *why* should inspire our *what*. When we all have shared purpose, we find that our success becomes greater. To have a vibrant and healthy culture, each person carries the charge to live a life full of purpose and passion. Knowing why we do what we do allows for greater purpose in our everyday work. The everyday "stuff" exists in every job; knowing why you do it is uncommon and most important. These ideas help guide us as individuals and as a company by challenging us to answer questions that impact who we are and what we do.

It's also about doing good at scale, not just a one-time event by a single person for only one day. It's about an entire organization of people focused on the sweet spot of the Culture of Good every day while recruiting others to participate in the journey with us at the same time.

In the next three chapters, we'll share some context for how the different parts of the Culture of Good operating system function together and how we made it work for us.

Questions to Consider
Scott's questions:

1. What is the company initiative that would tie your cause to your customers and your employees? Why do you think they would get behind it?

2. What would happen if you put a piece of one month's budget, say, your marketing spend, to something about your organization's cause instead?

Ryan's questions:

1. How might you go about rallying your people to a common cause?

2. Are there opportunities to build on good deeds and initiatives you already have in place in your organization or the company you work for?

Cause Matters

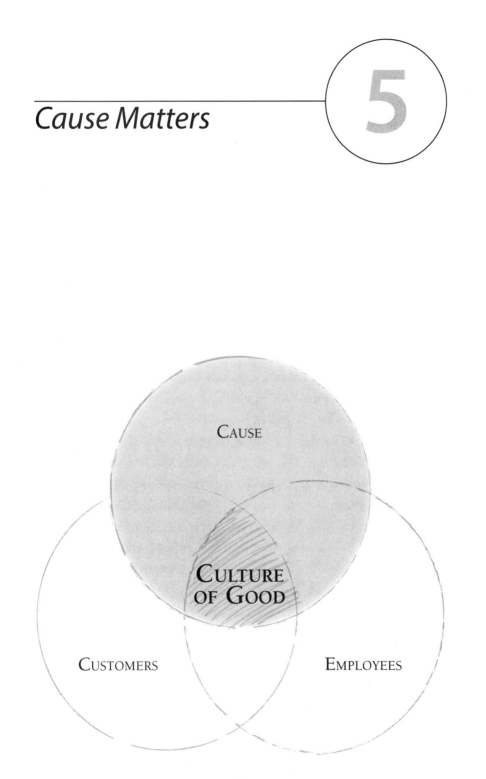

That first backpack giveaway built us a ton of momentum in pursuing the cause of organization: making communities better. While your organization may have a different cause from ours, the key is that the people in your organization are truly **passionate** about it. That's how you will win their hearts and minds.

The incredible thing for us is that the success of that first backpack initiative has only led to bigger and better things in our own making communities better efforts, particularly our four annual community-contribution campaigns, all of which have become part of our Culture of Good movement. TCC has now given back more than $9 million to our communities, a 500 percent increase from our first year of embracing the notion that communities were the common cause to bring our employees and customers together. (In fact, a portion of the sales of this book will be given to local charities, which will be chosen by each of our stores' employees.) The backpacks melted hearts. But if they were a one-time or once-a-year event, then people would forget about them. We'd all go on with our lives. What our challenge then became was how we could build on that and continue it by developing a cadence and making it more than just an annual event. We also needed a way to tackle the challenge of giving our people a chance to connect with that cause at different levels. If the backpack giveaway was an enterprise-level effort, we also needed to create ways for people to connect with the cause at regional or group levels, such as within a store, and as individuals, where they would be given permission to care about areas where they were personally passionate.

That's why we created more activities and encouraged people to get involved, such as:

1. **Teachers Rock Supply Giveaway**: At the beginning of each year, TCC donates school supply packs filled with glue, pencils, pens, markers, erasers, paper, tissue boxes, and more to 5,000 teachers across the country.

2. **Heal the World Environmental Campaign**: From April to June, TCC partners with local parks and organizations that care for the environment. At our initial launch of the initiative, we planted more than 5,000 trees in urban gardens and parks across the country.

3. **School Rocks Backpack Giveaway**: At the beginning of each school year, TCC donates 135,000 backpacks filled with school supplies to students throughout TCC's local communities. To date, TCC has donated 395,000 backpacks to children in need.

4. **Stop the Hunger Campaign**: In November and December, more than 500 TCC stores collect canned and boxed foods from customers and community members to provide to local partnering food banks. In November 2015, for instance, we collectively donated more than eight tons of food.

The beauty of this movement we have kicked off is that our associates all over the company have picked up the ball and begun doing good in their own special ways. We found that it was no longer just the "Scott and Ryan Show." We started to have individual people from all over the company step up and find their own way to contribute to our shared cause that community matters. Nothing builds employee engagement like shared values! More than 93 percent of our people feel that we share their values for social responsibility. We've had 58 percent of our folks hashtag at least one picture with #cultureofgood from a COG event, and more than 83 percent have used some or all of their 16 hours of paid volunteer time in their communities.

For example, we had Kattina Hantz, the store manager in Angola, Indiana, challenge her team to "change the world" over the holidays by doing whatever they could to truly make a positive impact on underprivileged families in her area.

After dropping off their Stop Hunger collections to Plum Food Pantry in December, the Angola and Auburn, Indiana, TCC stores realized that their support was needed beyond this single food drive. To make the greatest impact on the nonprofit, the stores combined their $125 quarterly donations and customer contributions and were able to spend $750 on gifts for two families that the food pantry connected them with for the holidays.

Five employees from the stores took the time to shop and wrap presents that were on the families' wish lists. Although the stores were hectic with last-minute holiday shoppers, each employee made it a priority to not only serve his or her customers but also make the holidays special for these local families in need.

Once the gifts were ready to be given, Kattina and her fellow teammates wanted to do more than just drop them off at Plum Food Pantry. On the Wednesday before Christmas Eve, they had the opportunity to deliver the gifts in-person to one of the families, who had five children. Kattina's fiancé, Mike Gephart, manager of the Auburn store, dressed as Santa Claus and stuffed the gifts in a sack.

The night the teams visited the family was a life-changing event. The kids hugged Santa and bounced with sheer joy on their new beanbag chairs. After Santa shook the father's hand to wish him a Merry Christmas, there was not a dry eye in the house. Everyone who was present that night walked away with a true understanding of the meaning of the holiday season.

Kattina has worked at TCC for 14 years, and this occasion was one of the best Culture of Good efforts she's ever experienced. She even brought her daughter to the family's home to show her how important it is to give back. "One of the biggest life lessons I try to teach my kids is the importance of helping those in need," says Kattina. "Not everyone can say they can do that through their jobs. But I am thankful to be able to instill these values in my own family through my work at TCC." The Angola and Auburn stores are looking forward to the next Culture of Good initiative so they can spread even more good throughout their communities.

Our Connection to Kids

Without a doubt, one of the causes that every member of the TCC family rallies for, connected to making communities better, is kids in need. That's why our backpack giveaway initiative has become such a success and why we have been drawn to support the teachers who have long looked out for their students, as Ryan's teacher Mrs. Overley had done so many years before. And while you might not realize it, most teachers reach into their own wallets and purses to pay for school supplies they need to help kids learn, which might include everything from presharpened pencils to Kleenex! So, similar to the backpack giveaway, our Teachers Rock initiative is a way for us to give back to those teachers who are always there for us when we need them the most.

Sharon O'Haver, a longtime TCC employee (and Scott's assistant), is just one employee who had an amazing experience with the Teachers Rock initiative. This is the e-mail she received after she had given a supply box to one of her kid's teachers:

OH MY GOODNESS! You are wonderful! What a thoughtful gift your company provides and at the perfect time in the school year! The box was full of so many things we run out of this time of year, and not only will I get plenty of use out of the supplies, but I can bless some other classroom/teachers who were just recently asking for some of the supplies (Kleenex and dry erase markers in particular :)).

continues ▷

> *Please let whoever is in charge of this wonderful initiative know how much we appreciate everything! It really is nice to know that someone appreciates the work we do at school and tries to help with some of the everyday items we teachers often buy for our classrooms!*
>
> *Thank you so much!*
>
> *Jessica*
>
> *(P.S. Whoever thought to add PRESHARPENED pencils just made my day!)*

On a similar note, it came very naturally to us to get involved with helping the kids at Riley Hospital for Children in Indianapolis beginning in August 2015. Each year, some 300,000 sick children visit Riley for help. It's an organization that Scott and his wife, Julie, have long been supporters of, which led them to a networking event where they made a pledge on behalf of TCC. But rather than just cutting a check, Scott and Ryan came up with a plan to tie the employees to the cause via the most mundane of items: screen-cleaning cloths. Every TCC store carried these innocuous cloths, but nobody ever really bought them. Scott's and Ryan's idea was to turn those items into ways to tell the stories of the kids at Riley by featuring artwork created by those kids. TCC would then sell those cloths in its stores with the end goal of then turning all those proceeds into a donation to the hospital.

One amazing result was that these cloths immediately gave our salespeople reasons to talk about our cause, and, by buying one of those cloths, a customer would be directly contributing to the Culture of Good by giving back to the sick kids in the community. Another incredible return was that we ended up raising a lot of money that we could donate to the hospital.

But rather than Scott taking the credit for that big donation, the key was to find a way for everyone in the company to play a role in giving back to the cause. That's when we came up with the crazy stupid idea of giving the hospital a hug. Wearing superhero costumes. Quite literally, 1,000 TCC employees dressed as Batman, Superman, and Spiderman joined together to link arms and embrace the hospital. The idea to dress up was inspired when we heard that the workers who washed the windows of the hospital would dress up in costumes, which gave the kids a thrill to see Spiderman climbing their building.

In our case, we had TCC employees fly in from 37 states for our first-ever Rally for Riley. When one person visits a children's hospital wearing a cape, that's a good deed. But when a thousand cape-wearing people come visit to lend some support to a bunch of sick children, that's when it's truly become a cause that fuels the Culture of Good. The kids were amazed. We had one little boy celebrating his birthday, and he was infatuated with Batman. When we found that out, we searched for the best-looking Batman to go up and talk to him. There were a lot of smiles and a lot of tears of joy.

TCC employees literally hugging Riley Hospital for Children.

We all gathered to help cheer up the kids and to share the news that we were donating $1 million to the hospital to fund Child Life and Social Service Programming, which included hiring three employees to run those programs for the kids. We also donated an additional $250,000 to fund a rain forest–themed art and activity room and help the hospital provide treatment to children whose families cannot afford it. The room will be a merging of rain forest and technology, which will include a projector with a screen where the kids can watch movies, as well as computer tablets so kids can watch videos and do homework.

A caped Scott celebrating his giant check moment: a $1 million donation to Riley Hospital for Children.

"We want to create a space where the patients can be kids, not feel like sick kids but kids with imagination," Ryan told *People*. At the end of the day, the superheroes, doctors, staff, and patients came together to join hands and "hug" the hospital. "It was just a really emotional moment because it signified our love for the kids and the doctors," Ryan said at the time. "We went there dressed up as superheroes, but we know the real superheroes are the kids."

And another one of those kids truly made an impact on everyone at TCC: 9-year-old Olivia Pierce. Olivia, who is wiser than her age, spoke to all of us there that day and told us how back when she was three months old, she was diagnosed with malignant tumors affecting both of her eyes. While chemotherapy shrunk the retinoblastoma tumors and saved her right eye, doctors were forced to remove her left eye. And Olivia and her doctors continue to fight to save her right eye. She has since undergone 35 surgeries at Riley Hospital for Children to help reduce the remaining tumors in her right eye, and her family remains confident in the care she continues to receive. Olivia's charisma and positivity as she talked about the struggle that she and the other patients at Riley Hospital face won over the hearts of every one of us, and we know for sure we shed more than a few tears as we shared in this young woman's pain.

But you might not know what she continues to struggle through if you meet her. Not only is Olivia wise but also she's spunky as hell. When she got the chance to address an audience of some 500 believers in the Culture of Good at a TCC sales rally in Chicago, she talked about her love of the Chicago Blackhawks. In fact, Olivia shared with everyone how she has a "tattoo," actually an engraving of the Hawks logo, on her artificial eye courtesy of some talented engravers. "I'm the biggest little Hawks fan in the world," Olivia said.

The events of that day at the hospital also hit close to home for Frank Gumino, chief information officer at TCC. Frank's 14-year-old daughter, Grace, is a Riley kid who recently finished chemotherapy after two and a half years of battling leukemia. While Frank had always sympathized with those affected by serious illness prior to the onset of his daughter's illness, he never truly understood the hardships that kids and families endure when a loved one is given a life-threating diagnosis. Standing outside Riley Hospital was an especially moving moment for him and his family because they had the firsthand knowledge of what goes on inside its doors.

Frank knew, for example, how the physicians at Riley Hospital have a real affection for the patients they're caring for, as well as for their families. His daughter's oncologist went so far as to give them his cell phone number in case they wanted to contact him directly with any concerns. When he then heard from Olivia about her difficult journey, Frank was especially touched and inspired.

"I'm not sure many of us would be able to do what the Riley kids do every day fighting disease," he says. "These kids are so strong and take on these battles with such a positive attitude. My daughter and kids like Olivia should cause us all to pause when we think we're having a bad day on the job or feeling some aches and pains. I am so proud to have been part of Rally for Riley, and I know everything that TCC is doing for the patients is helping them feel like happy, normal kids."

What that day at Riley also helped cement for Frank was that our company truly practices what it preaches when it comes to giving back and supporting local communities. He even remembers when, right after he joined the company, he wrapped up one of his first presentations to the executive team and Scott asked him why the Culture of Good wasn't a part of his message. It was then that Frank knew he had made the right decision to work for a company that puts doing good on the same level as running the business.

Yousif Baghdadi, store manager in River Forest, Illinois, was also moved by the check donation and human chain formed at Riley Hospital. Dressed as a huge cat alongside his fellow employees who sported Scooby-Doo, Garfield, and Tigger costumes, Yousif met Olivia and had the opportunity to put a smile on the face of another Riley patient who came outside to see what all the excitement was about. The two joined hands and danced together, and it was a feeling Yousif will never forget. In fact, he describes the moment as an epiphany. "Spending time with those kids and hearing their stories motivated me to do whatever I can to help support Riley Hospital," he says.

In fact, Yousif has become a huge supporter of the initiative we started where Riley kids such as Olivia create some eye-popping original designs that we use to make our phone-screen wipes, which we call awesome cloths. These cloths have become our highest-selling accessory, and 100 percent of the profits go to funding new programs at Riley. What's incredible is that even though TCC associates don't make a dime on the sale of these cloths, they are incredibly passionate about sparking conversations with their customers about why buying them matters so much to kids like Olivia in their communities. "For me, it all starts with selling as many Riley screen cloths in my store as possible," says Yousif, whose store is one of more than 350 across the country that are selling awesome cloths. So far, Yousif's team has sold 160 screen cloths to customers, totaling $1,600 raised for Riley Hospital in less than two months and making it one of the very best examples of what happens when you give people permission to care and build the Culture of Good.

Since Yousif was the only employee from his store present at the rally, Olivia wanted to personally meet and thank the other River Forest employees for their dedication to raising money for Riley kids. She visited the store a couple of weekends ago, bringing her story to life for the employees who had not yet met her.

Meeting Olivia felt extremely personal to River Forest employee Jeremy Johnson, who is leading the store in selling the most screen cloths. "Years ago, my little brother spent a few weeks at a children's hospital in Chicago," he says.

"I remember how awesome the staff was in making him feel like he wasn't at a hospital and was just a regular kid. Selling the Riley screen cloths is so important for me, as it gives me a chance to give back to other kids who are going through an experience similar to what my brother endured."

For Yousif, Jeremy, and the rest of the River Forest staff, raising money for a hospital that isn't local does not matter when it comes to doing good. Selling the screen cloths to support sick children is what's important to them because it's the right thing to do. "Selling the screen cloths is a pretty simple process because our customers want to help," Yousif says. "We are already recognized by our customers for giving back to the community, so when we tell them that 100 percent of their screen cloth purchase is going to a great cause, they believe in us."

The impact goes both ways as well. When Scott pulled aside another one of the young ladies who had crafted a design for one of the awesome cloths, he asked her whether she knew that her design would be sold in stores all around the country. Immediately, her mouth dropped open and she turned to her parents and said, "I am going to be famous!"

What We Learned about Why Cause Matters

We've shared our story about how we found the cause that our employees and customers rallied around to create our Culture of Good: making communities better. And we learned an important lesson along that journey. The question is, what is the cause your organization will rally around? When you think about it, most businesses start as a way to solve a problem or fill a need. You have a real sense of purpose—a **why**—when you pursue a goal like that. That's why you see so many people drawn to work at startups: they are energized by the idea that they are making the world better for their customers and their cause even in some small way.

But what happens so often in business is that as the organization grows and adds more people and customers and moves into new towns and cities, it begins to forget about those core values that made the place so special when it started. The mission shifts from filling that need to fine-tuning a spreadsheet. You move from thinking three dimensionally to taking on a two-dimensional view of the world, where you've extracted emotion and purpose from the equation. It's why people feel like robots or numbers when they work for big corporations. They wish they could get back to working at a place where they felt like they made a real difference in the world.

They know they've lost something, but they can't quite put their finger on what is missing.

To try to fill that void, companies start CSR initiatives or other programs as a way to give back. And what happens is that the organization does some good either by raising a bunch of money and stroking a check or in getting their employees to donate their time to a good cause. But this isn't culture change. It's a patch that usually doesn't stick over the long term. Eventually, it just fails. But why is that?

We met a woman, a friend of a friend, who has worked with some of the biggest and most well-known companies in the world on building CSR programs. In one case, she shared a story with us about how she was hired by the CEO of a global bank to implement a program that would support the environment. It was a passion of his, and he invested millions of dollars of the bank's money in rolling out this program. But guess what? While it did do some good in the short term and plenty of people inside the bank donated their money and time to the cause, it eventually sputtered out. Over time, people lost interest in this program because it was completely off the crosshairs of what they did on a daily basis. They had no way of tying what they did in their jobs to the cause of protecting the environment. A real disconnect exists between the worlds of banking and rain forests. This was more about the CEO rolling out a pet project and then hammering it into place, where, in time, it began to rot away. The company still hadn't found what was really at its soul.

We don't mean to pick on this bank, but it helps paint the context of what finding your company's soul is really all about. You can't just pluck some cause out of thin air and then drop it into your organization and expect everyone to embrace it. If we had tried to do something similar at TCC, we would have arrived at the same result. Our employees would have told us to go shove it because it wasn't authentic. If we told our customers that we were donating money from every purchase to save trees in Brazil, they would have told us to screw off, too. They can't make the connection. There's no there, there. It doesn't come across as authentic. That's not what the soul of our company is about.

When we look back at the history of our business, we see that it started in rural regions as a way to service local communities where we were the only phone store in town. Our mom-and-pop stores were important hubs in the communities we served. We lived our Midwestern values. We created jobs for people who liked to interact and help the people in their communities. Our customers loved us. We mattered. We still do!

What we have come to realize is that was the core of our company's soul. It was about doing good by people: our employees, our customers, and the members of the communities we live and work in. That's why people want to work for our company and why customers want to buy from us—because they know we are a part of the community.

But as we began to grow and add more stores and new people around the country, we began to lose sight of that. We began to look at our spreadsheets more than into our hearts. We almost lost our soul.

It's not like we weren't trying to do good all along. Scott even tried to launch a program where the business would partner with local schools to help them raise money. The idea was to give coupons to schools that would distribute them to parents and staff to use when shopping at our stores. Then, the company would donate a portion of every sale made—$10 for every phone or $4 for every accessory—back to the school. The school could then use that money for anything it wanted, such as saving a music program or hiring a gym teacher. No strings attached. It sounded like a win-win for everyone. Sure, the company would make some money, but it was truly about helping the kids. Scott fully expected dozens of schools to participate. But you know what happened? Not a single school signed up.

Not a one. They didn't want to touch that program with a 12-foot-pole. It didn't connect to our soul.

But we got lucky. We met each other in time to find what had been missing. We got lucky because we started an initiative, the backpack give-away, that rekindled that connection between our employees and the soul of the business. We gave our people the permission to care again as part of their jobs. The reason our Culture of Good works, and why a CSR program to save the environment would fail, is because we found those core beliefs that had been the foundation of our business all along.

Another lesson we learned relates to how you can embrace financial creativity when it comes to connecting to a meaningful cause. Certainly, we get asked a lot about whether a company or organization, especially a smaller one with less resources than TCC has, needs to spend the kind of money we did on, say, our backpack initiative, in order for this to work. The quick answer is no, you don't have to spend oodles of money on this to make it work. Money helps, of course. But we also could have found alternative and more creative ways to help launch and sponsor the different initiatives that went into our own flavor of the Culture of Good. We could have, for example, reached out to different vendors and asked them to partner with us or asked whether they would participate in a matching-contribution program. That would have been a great way to get our business partners to commit to a shared vision with us and also get them engaged in doing good while at the same time sharing in the financial investment to make it all work. That's an easy win-win for everyone.

We also learned that we were wasting some pretty valuable resources on what we thought was effective marketing. Whenever we opened a new store, for instance, we gave that store $8,000 to get the word out by doing everything from placing ads in newspapers and on the radio to renting a blow-up animal of some kind to attract attention. A popcorn machine almost always showed up, too. All fun stuff, right? Sure. But then we thought about it differently. We asked ourselves what would happen if we took that same budget and allowed our customers to tell us what local charities they would like to see us support with that instead. And do you know what happened? Our customers loved the idea so much that our stores got far more traction than any ad we could have bought. Even better, we allowed them to vote for their top three charities, each of which got a share of that $8,000 we used to spend on popcorn.

The point is that kicking off a Culture of Good doesn't mean you have to come up with new funding sources. Maybe it starts with looking at areas you already have money in the budget for, such as marketing efforts, and repurposing them to do some good for your customers, your communities, and your employees in order to hit that sweet spot at the center of the Culture of Good. Consider that some food for thought.

As far as what we might have done differently if we could do it all over again, we would have embraced the idea of the Culture of Good from day one, as opposed to creating something ourselves and then asking our employees to join in. By doing it differently, we could have given our people the reassurance that this wasn't about introducing another program but instead a way of life tied to our wanting to change how we went about our work.

Questions to Consider
Scott's questions:

1. When you define your cause effort, are you meeting the trends of your customers and employees?

2. How transparent are you about your cause? Do your employees and customers understand how you help them connect to it?

Ryan's questions:

1. How confident are you that each of your employees understands your cause and can explain it to your customers?

2. How important is it for you to know the cause of the companies that you purchase from or do business with?

3. Are you more apt to do business with someone who has a cause you know about versus some place where you don't know its cause?

Making Employees Better

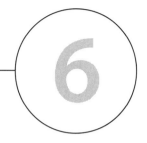

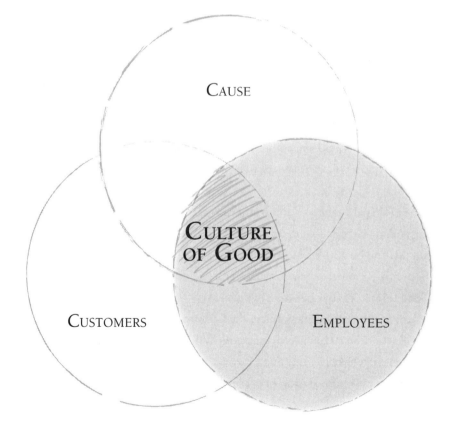

Once you understand **why** *you* do **what** you do, the next step is identifying who in your organization should be given the permission to care. That's why a key element to hitting the sweet spot of the Culture of Good is to ensure that your employees truly connect with your organizational cause. But when you consider that people can connect with a cause at three different levels—enterprise, region/group, and individual—you can't always drive that engagement with the cause throughout the organization from the top down. You can't just hang up a poster, send out an e-mail, or make a clever video. You can't grab people's hearts and minds by appealing only to their eyeballs or their funny bones. You can't build a great culture with great furniture and cool toys, even if a kegerator every Friday afternoon sounds amazing.

Rather, we have learned that to build that connection between our employees and our cause—making communities better for TCC—we needed to give autonomy to individual employees and local stores in implementing events and choosing local charities. We're now creating autonomy for individuals who have embraced the Culture of Good as a way to truly scale the impact we can have as an organization. We have created a way for our employees to have a voice in what cause we pursue and how, rather than those efforts always being run from the top down. "Running this by myself has taught me that I can't run this by myself," says Ryan. "The employees run this and own it. We have to trust our employees to do good themselves." To put that another way, we finally learned about how to turn the Culture of Good from a "fly-by-the-seat-of-your-pants" kind of thing to an operational system within our business where the Culture of Good is woven into every single action we take as an organization. While we're not perfect, nor will we ever be, we've evolved and put a process in place where we use dashboards and metrics to measure the impact we're having, just like we do with our financials.

To maintain company consistency, we define and supply the products that will be given away on the day of an event such as the backpack giveaway. We then leave the planning of the event to the stores, including the opportunity for the stores to choose which local charities they want to donate money to. For example, some stores have created very successful block parties with DJs and events that involve the whole community. Every year, employees are also given 16 hours of paid time off to volunteer, whether that volunteer time is during work hours or not. Employees are also free to contribute ideas to grow the effort. A recent batch of new hires were asking about a recycling initiative, for instance, so we responded by sending money to each store to start a recycle initiative or whatever effort they chose to make the greatest positive impact on their local environment.

Another practice we've come to appreciate is finding ways to get the people in our stores—you know, the ones who are the real face of our company—together at least once a year to connect and get reenergized. Many companies hold events like these, of course. They're called sales rallies or annual meetings, and the focus is usually on setting financial goals and targets everyone needs to meet. We have taken a different tact. When we get our people together, we spare them the beating of the drum to meet their targets. They get enough of that in their daily routines. What we do instead is use these opportunities to get our people excited and pumped up about the Culture of Good and their **why** rather than just their **what**.

We got amazing reactions, for example, when we held a rally in Chicago that we called Unleashed, where we invited 500 frontline sales people to participate in two days of personal development and, yes, some partying while their managers stayed home. The late-night entertainment involved a dance party fueled by the rocking raps of Chanel West Coast, who flew in after her performance at the Coachella music festival. Burn, managers.

More importantly, this was our opportunity to speak to our young workforce and show them how much the company cared about them and their ability to grow both as professionals and as people. They got to hear a very personal and moving speech from Erik Schlesselman, the chief revenue officer at TCC, who shared how he started in the same front-line position that every person in the audience had. And, over time, Erik moved up through the ranks by taking advantage of all the opportunities TCC offered him. "Opportunity isn't always convenient," Erik told us. "But I came to believe that we need others to succeed. And when we win together, success becomes more fulfilling. We all want to be part of something bigger than ourselves. And when we fight together for a common cause, that's how we become a family."

It shouldn't come as a shock that we also used this event as an opportunity to do a lot of good toward our organizational cause, which, in this case, involved creating more than 1,000 play kits that we donated to the Lurie Children's Hospital in Chicago that is part of the same Children's Miracle Network that Riley also belongs to. And, oh, yeah, we also donated $10,000 to Lurie on behalf of our people. "Your hard work is what allows us to make miracles happen," Scott told the audience.

Another great moment during the rally happened when Scott randomly brought on stage a TCC employee named Josiah Kirton. Scott asked Josiah, who was 22 at the time, about where he lived: Gaithersburg, Maryland—the same town of 3,000 residents he grew up in. Josiah said he came to work for TCC because he knew it was family owned. "And in family-owned companies, people matter," he told those of us in the audience. Since then, Josiah became somewhat of a go-to resource, a trusted advisor, for his community when it came to solving problems with their phones. Whenever he went out to eat, for example, he was constantly being asked to fix something on someone's phone, a role he relished.

When Scott asked Josiah what kept him working for TCC, aside from the paycheck, he said it was his chance to give back to his hometown community. "I care about the place I grew up in," Josiah said. That's also why, when Scott asked him to share a Making Communities Better experience that was most near and dear to his heart, Josiah said he most enjoyed the Teachers Rock initiative. "It's been an honor to give back to those teachers who gave so much to us," Josiah said. To thank Josiah for his enthusiasm and his desire to do so much good, Scott decided on the spot to give Josiah $2,500 to run a Teachers Rock initiative in whatever way he wanted to. As Scott and Josiah exchanged a big old bear hug, the walls just about fell down in the wake of the raucous applause and cheers that erupted from the crowd. And it doesn't end there, as every time we hold a rally, it builds on the last one. We build more awareness about our cause and how our employees can engage with it and ultimately help our customers connect with it as well.

It's Not for Everyone (Or Is It?)

To make the Culture of Good sustainable over the long term is, as the great Jim Collins puts it, ensuring that you have the right people on the bus. That's especially powerful when you consider that the primary reason people stay at their jobs is when they have three friends who work there as well. And if you work with as many millennials as we do in our business, embracing a concept as powerful as the Culture of Good, something that helps you build relationships with your coworkers, it certainly becomes a major factor in engagement and retention. Some 92 percent of our employees tell us that the Culture of Good gives them a sense of fulfillment. While only 44 percent of employees initially chose to work at TCC because of our Culture of Good, more than 82 percent of our people say it is a contributing factor in staying here. And we'll be honest: retaining people in the retail industry ain't easy.

We have identified that within the industry, a lot of people leave around the six-month mark. So we make a point of celebrating everyone who reaches that mark with TCC. We even host a special quarterly two-day event at headquarters, where we fly anyone who reaches the six-month milestone to our offices outside of Indianapolis. And it's not just managers and assistant managers who we fly out either; it's everyone. Then, during their two days, they meet with folks at TCC to learn more about the company, meet its leaders in person, and experience more of where the Culture of Good first began, all as a way to get them more closely aligned with the why behind it. We do all this because employees matter and we want to invite them to join our cause. And if they stay, that's worth celebrating. For what it's worth, it's also good for the long-term health of the business because we've got a turnover rate that is half the industry average.

In surveys with our employees, we have found that 80 percent of those who are between 35 and 50 years old, our Gen Xers and baby boomers, say that the Culture of Good is a contributing factor to continuing employment at TCC. But 92 percent of those who are between the ages of 25 and 35, our millennials, say that our culture is a major factor in their choosing to work for our company. One employee even proudly posted on Facebook a few of the big wins she had experienced in her time at TCC. Incredibly, her post almost seemed to go viral with her friends; many posted comments along the lines of "Damn, I wish my company would do stuff like that."

We've also implemented active policies to help further drive that engagement between our employees and our cause. Case in point: 50 percent of every employee's performance review is based on how he or she reflects the three pillars of the Culture of Good. That's right: we review our people on how much they live out in practice what we're preaching. And sometimes that takes some reminding. Frank Gumino, TCC's CIO, who was moved by our experience with Riley Hospital, could have worked anywhere, but he ultimately chose to work with us because he felt so passionate about our culture. However, when Frank went to his first performance review with Scott, he came prepared with everything but what he had done to show how he had helped connect his team to the cause.

Stories like this really help illustrate how we are injecting the Culture of Good into our company's DNA because it's not a side note—it's literally at the core of everything we do. It's not a patch we've sewn onto the outside of the organization. Rather, as we make business decisions, it makes up the pillars of the Culture of Good that govern the direction we take, more so than even how much revenue or profit we might make. Again, we're not saying you can ignore financial sustainability. We're just saying that we won't sacrifice our culture or its values to achieve a two-dimensional goal.

We've also evolved our recruiting strategies to incorporate the Culture of Good as a value. If candidates are not ready to do good as part of their work, we simply tell them that TCC won't be a good fit for them. By doing so, TCC is attracting talent that is a better fit with the culture and more likely to stay longer.

That notion has been validated by people such as John Baldoni, an executive coach with the firm N2Growth and a best-selling author himself, who has worked with hundreds of companies over his career and seen just about every flavor of culture that exists. "But what you guys are doing with your culture is special," John has told us. "Most people, especially millennials, are looking for meaning in their work; they want to do something different. You're giving them that opportunity by giving them the chance to be inspired and to give back while they work. This resonates with people, and they are attracted to it or they opt out."

A great example of this dynamic is Mitchell Sprouse, a sales rep from the central New York State town of Pulaski. As Mitchell told us, he first heard about our Culture of Good when he applied for his job. When he heard stories about it, he thought working for TCC might be more than just another job. "I lost my best friend to cancer when he was 19 years old," Mitchell told us. "I had seen a lot of young kids going through chemo, so I had a passion to be able to help kids out. I was starting to feel like I was being pulled away from TCC for my family and for a chance at more money. My wife told me money wasn't everything, and I knew that."

Mitchell admits that when he attended our sales rally that April, he was really looking for something to keep him working at TCC. Well, wouldn't you know it, but that little lady Olivia struck again: "When Olivia was on stage talking, I felt that same drive again," Mitchell told us. "Later that evening, I was privileged and blessed to meet her and her mother. It was at that moment everything came full circle and I knew this right here was my calling. It's not about the sales and the money. It's about being at a place where I am treated like family, a place where I can be happy and do good every day. For kids like Olivia and anyone else, the Culture of Good impacts. I felt something change right then, and then when Ryan spoke, I knew everything was confirmed. I actually started tearing up during his speech just because I knew what I was doing mattered. I can't wait to spread the joy of COG to my market and my community. The smallest spark can ignite the biggest fire."

What we've found so far in listening to supporters such as Mitchell is that embracing the values of the Culture of Good turns people on way more than it turns them off. In fact, we've found that our culture is a big part of why we've been able to throw gasoline on our growth rate because we've been able to attract superstar talents such as Omar Khan, who joined TCC as its president in 2015.

Before joining TCC, Omar spent more than three years as co-CEO of NQ Mobile, a global provider of consumer and enterprise mobile Internet services. Before that, he was Citigroup's managing director and global head of the Mobile Center of Excellence, leading the company's mobile development efforts. But his résumé doesn't stop there. He also held several senior roles at Samsung Mobile, including chief strategy officer and chief product and technology officer. And even before that, Omar spent eight years at Motorola, where he was a VP of global supply chain and business operations for the mobile devices business. In short, this guy is a stud who knows the mobile business inside and out.

So why would a guy like this (and also like Frank), someone who could work just about anywhere in the world, come take a job at TCC? Let's just say our company culture played a pivotal role.

Omar first learned about TCC when he met Scott and Julie at a global wireless conference in Barcelona a few years back. He and Scott hit it off right away. Not only do they share a birthday but also they are both ambidextrous. Eventually, TCC became a customer of Omar's company, and the two stayed in close touch over the next few years. Scott would call Omar every now and again and bounce some ideas off him about his vision for TCC and where the wireless retail business was headed. Scott valued Omar's insights and found out during their many conversations that he also had the ability to just about finish Scott's sentences for him. As Omar puts it, he "speaks Scott."

Another topic that Omar and Scott would keep coming back to was how they could work together more. Eventually, Scott cut to the chase: he asked Omar to come work at TCC. So why did Omar say yes?

"Because I knew Scott was someone I would enjoy working with," says Omar. "But I knew that if I took another job, I wanted it to be somewhere where I felt like I had a vested interest in the future of the business. It had to be more than about a paycheck. I wanted the chance to leave a mark on the community and industry we are part of, to build a legacy that we as a company would be proud of for years to come."

While Omar and his family had been active in giving back to charities and volunteering their time for good causes away from work, he saw the potential of helping stoke the fires of the Culture of Good at TCC. "It is about building a lifetime relationship with employees and caring about things beyond a paycheck or a financial transaction by connecting with communities," says Omar. "It's about being passionate about doing good and how that creates loyalty among employees and customers. Choosing to work at TCC was about giving me the chance to build on that foundation and get real satisfaction from my work."

What's funny is that Omar told Scott he planned on taking six months off to relax before he joined TCC. He ended up starting 10 days after he left his prior gig because he just couldn't wait to get started. "Coming to work at a place like TCC is a joy; it doesn't feel like work," says Omar. "Yes, I love my family and the time we have together at home. But you know you have found something special when you can come to work every day and it satisfies your soul."

Omar isn't the only one who feels drawn to the special sauce we're cooking up at TCC. That's why the Culture of Good is now an essential part of our new-hire onboarding process. We've been amazed to see how folks immediately take to it. As an example, consider this e-mail Ryan received from a new TCC employee named Deliah:

> *Hello,*
>
> *My name is Deliah, and I am part of the training class you just spoke to. I just wanted to take the time to thank you for speaking and tell you that not only have you changed my entire perspective of this company, but you have left a mark on my life I won't soon forget. Thank you for showing me that TCC thinks of us as people and not just an employee. Thank you for sharing your story and reminding us that we are not alone. You are a wonderful representation of TCC and Moorehead Communications as a whole, and I am very*

grateful to be a part of this team. I wish you luck in all your endeavors and again, thank you.

Sincerely, Deliah

We can't tell you how validating and moving it is to receive notes like this. Thank you, Deliah and Omar, for letting us know that we're on the right path.

Keeping the Right People

On a similar note, part of the growth strategy in our business has been to acquire other companies in our space. The challenge with that strategy is that we are also asking dozens, hundreds, or even thousands of new people to join our Culture of Good. It's well known in the business world that while acquisitions might look good on paper, if you don't engage the hearts and minds of the people involved in those mergers, you're inheriting more trouble than anything else. That's why so many mergers fail to pay off over the long run.

But we have a secret weapon when tackling this challenge: our Culture of Good. Consider that we made a series of acquisitions in 2015, which included a dozen stores operating in Pennsylvania. John Cooper, TCC's director of operations, who, at the time, was the district manager of operations of those newly acquired stores in northern Pennsylvania, says that immersing new employees into TCC's culture is critical to ongoing organizational triumphs. He credits his fellow employees for the smooth transition. "It's normal for new employees to feel some level of stress and anxiety," says John, who originally started at TCC as a frontline salesperson. "Thankfully, nerves were quickly replaced by excitement when our new employees learned about TCC's Culture of Good. Each of them could not wait to be part of something bigger than him- or herself."

John says that he is personally excited by the changes in the culture he has seen during his time with TCC. While he always enjoyed the family feel that the Mooreheads had imparted from the beginning, he feels that the Culture of Good was a big leap forward in terms of connecting employees and their families with the customers and the communities where they operate. That includes the start of manager-in-training programs that give TCC employees the opportunity to learn the skills they need to advance their careers. "We are moving out of the mind-set that we are a wireless retail store to one where we offer our people a career where they can learn and develop," says John.

But the really special sauce, John says, is when you add the level of passion and engagement like you see when people participate in their first backpack giveaway; that's truly special. "I am so excited to see where this goes from here," says John, who moved from Pennsylvania to Indiana to pursue his own calling within TCC. "My dream is to hear that 10 years from now, someone comes up to us and tells us, 'You changed my life when I was a kid.'"

The Culture of Good has also helped reunite us with great employees such as Amber Back, who needed to leave the company. In Amber's case, she decided to leave TCC to fulfill a promise she made to her dying mother to get her degree. The decision was tough because Amber loved her job as the assistant manager of our store in Lebanon, Indiana. When she left, her manager made it clear that she would be welcome back if she ever wanted to return.

Fast-forward a few years. Amber made good on her promise to her mom—in fact, she doubled it by earning degrees in both interior design technology and psychology. But when she started interviewing for jobs at different design firms, she felt out of place. "They all felt so tight-laced," says Amber. "I couldn't find an environment that felt comfortable to be in. I had a gut feeling that I wouldn't be happy there."

As a way to earn money while she figured out her career, which now included a real estate license, Amber thought she could go back to slinging phones. But when she went back to visit the store in Lebanon, she realized how much had changed in the six years she had been gone. Not only had the name of the company changed to TCC but also she learned how much bigger the business had become. She also started hearing about this thing called the Culture of Good. While she had enjoyed the family atmosphere that existed with the Cellular Connection before, what she saw at TCC now was something altogether different. "It began to dawn on me that so many things had helped the company evolve into something a lot bigger that also had a much different feel than when I last worked there," says Amber.

Those changes really hit home when she participated in her new-hire training, something that hadn't existed in her prior stint with the company. She remembers how Scott, wearing cargo shorts and a T-shirt, walked into the training room and plopped himself down on a table in front of the group, his sandaled feet dangling before him. He then proceeded to use every curse word in the book. "I sat there and thought, 'Wow, this is the last thing anyone would expect from a CEO of a company this large,'" says Amber.

Amber says she got even more excited about TCC when she got the chance to see Scott and Ryan in action at a town hall meeting held in Indianapolis a few months later. There, over a hearty dinner, she was inspired hearing Scott's goal to make TCC the "biggest damn small company on the planet." Just as importantly, she connected with the goals of the Culture of Good and the movement that Scott and Ryan are trying to build around it.

"It shows employees that they matter," she says. "It also encourages us and others working with TCC to get involved and to give back, because everyone's life matters. The more we succeed as a company, the more we can use the Culture of Good to give back. Most companies just don't do this. They are more focused on bringing in money than they are on making life better. It's extremely inspiring to be part of. It's clear I was meant to work here."

After that evening, Amber actually posted a moving Facebook post to sum up her experience:

> *After working here for three years and being gone for six, this is why I came back to TCC last year. This is a company that cares. I cannot stress enough how wonderful people are nor how deeply they care about people and their healthy, joyful well-being. This is a company that cares and strives to be better each and every day. At the end of our dinner this evening we were challenged to each describe the day with one word. I chose a noun: **Possibility**. They listen, and then they react in productive, helpful ways. Scott has made this into a flexible, adaptive movement. This company has grown leaps and bounds, and I am confident that we will continue to do so. I could not work for a company that did not invest in its people, their work environment, and the lives of others around the world. I've thought of one more word: **Proud**.*

It's a Calling

Concerning your people, another lesson worth imparting is that building a Culture of Good is a gift to those you work with as much as it is a benefit to your organizational cause or your customers. Consider that employees these days, especially millennials, change jobs as frequently as every three to six months! Why? It's not because they're greedy or spoiled. Millennials are changing jobs because they want to find work that means something, work with a greater purpose that makes a difference. They want to find their *calling*.

But what do most companies offer? Jobs, right? And that's worth something, no doubt. We need jobs as a way to provide food and shelter for our families and ourselves. The rub is that when people just do a job, they're not really in it for more than those basic needs. You're not getting their best effort because they're always looking forward to the end of their shift or to the weekend so they can spend time doing something they actually *want* to do. People who are working for a job will do just enough not to get fired. And, as an employer, you will pay them just enough so that they won't quit. Both sides are leaving something on the table.

Now, some companies do a better job addressing this gap by finding ways to offer their employees a *career*: a ladder to secure more lucrative and rewarding work. Careers also offer more security than mere jobs do; you have a sense that you are needed and that you can count on getting paid every two weeks. You're also more likely to put in extra effort, such as working on evenings and weekends because you value the added benefits your employer is giving you in exchange for a reasonable salary. But even with all these benefits, a career still lacks something—that personal connection to something you care deeply about and are passionate about.

That's why if you, as an employer, can create an opportunity for your employees to pursue a *calling* through their work, well, you've done something special. The same applies if you, as an employee, have found something special about the place you go to work at every day. And we're not talking about a religious experience here (though that might apply to some of you). Rather, this is about giving your people the chance to rethink and reimagine what they do by challenging them to identify why they do it. Instead of *working*, they are *serving*. This gets to the root of that third dimension of business—feelings—that Scott talks about. When you are serving someone versus working, it's easy to get inspired and truly feel the sense of purpose that engulfs you. It gets to the very root of WHY you're doing your WHAT: to be part of something greater than yourself. This is exactly the foundation that nonprofits rely on to attract and engage people. Why shouldn't it also apply to a for-profit operation? If you're able, you can truly differentiate yourself in the market. Whom do you think purpose-minded employees would rather work for? The same goes for your customers: do you think they'd rather interact with people working at a job or those serving their calling? The answer is obvious.

Think about the timeless story of the three bricklayers: A man comes upon a construction site where three people are working. He asks the first, "What are you doing?" and the man replies, "I am laying bricks." He asks the second, "What are you doing?" and the man replies, "I am building a wall." As he approaches the third, he hears him humming a tune as he works. So he asks him the same question, "What are you doing?" The man stands, looks up at the sky, and smiles as he replies, "I am building a cathedral!"

The idea that we all want to pursue a calling rather than merely work a job gets to the very root of giving people permission to care. While the two of us spar from time to time about what the Culture of Good really means (Is it about a way to run a company, or is it about a way to engage people?), we do agree on a connection: you can't find your company's soul until you help your employees find theirs first. That's what the Culture of Good is all about. As Ryan says, "We find our calling when our greatest passion collides with our greatest contribution to make the world better."

But, again, don't trust just us. We admittedly were both caught off guard when we received the following note from Ashley Rapoza, a sales rep in a store outside Seattle, after she attended our Unleashed rally in Chicago. Here's what she had to tell us:

> *When I began working at TCC, no one on my team knew*
> *it, but I was homeless. I stayed from place to place, and*

sometimes when I had nowhere to go, I would just ride the buses around Seattle all night until I needed to head to work the next day. Most of the food I ate came from a local food bank that I was comfortable going to. The staff was friendly and never asked uncomfortable questions. Within my first two checks at TCC, I was able to get an apartment close to work that I only needed to take one bus to commute. Through the COG at my store, I have been able to donate money, food, and time to the food bank that helped me during my rough points in life. I came from a very low-income family growing up and was helped by many nonprofits growing up including the Salvation Army and Camp Orca. Through the COG initiative my store has planned how my team and I will be able to help out both these organizations in the next few months so they can continue to help families like mine. My ultimate goal for the COG would be to help fund Camp Orca and send a few energetic reps to volunteer as counselors. Camp Orca is a nonprofit summer camp for kids that provides a summer camp experience for kids whose families couldn't afford it otherwise. Most the staff is volunteers, and most the funding is donated money. It means so much to the kids who attend and was one of my happiest experiences growing up. TCC is probably the only company I have worked for who cares about who I am as a person and how I can grow. My district managers help me grow beyond my numbers; they genuinely care about me growing as a leader. This is a company I want to grow with.

Wow, right? When Scott first read this, he started crying. Ashley's story just hits home the power of giving people permission to care and to give back in ways they are most passionate about. That's the difference between going to work at a job or even to pursue a career. What Ashley has found is her calling, and we're beyond proud to support her in any way that we can.

Lessons from Our Journey

When you look at where we did the most good in the early years of the Culture of Good, we see now that we focused mostly on the communities in which we operated. That's largely because that's where Ryan's expertise was and where he knew how to make an impact. And there is nothing wrong with that. It's just that our cause is only one component of the Culture of Good. What we learned, especially in the wake of the first back-pack giveaway, was that we had perhaps overlooked how we could have helped some of our employees as much as the members of our community or even our customers. Employees make up our internal community, and when we learned that some of them could have used backpacks for their kids, well, we were somewhat humbled to recognize that we had perhaps overlooked our own people at times. How can we ask our employees to care about our customers and endorse our cause that communities matter if they don't feel cared for where they work? Obviously, we can't. We made the mistake of allowing our cause to overshadow our commitment that our employees matter equally. Fortunately, we learned this lesson early enough to make corrections by building systems that would allow our people to ask for help when they needed it. Again, we have been far from perfect at times. But what makes the Culture of Good really special in our organization is our ability and willingness to learn and change as we continue to evolve.

Another key lesson we learned is that building the Culture of Good can't be just one person's job, even if he or she is a superstar like Ryan. While you need buy-in from the top leaders in the organization, the movement takes on so much more power when it comes from many people throughout the organization.

To meet the need of getting buy-in across all layers of the company, we tried to implement a program we called the Champions program. The idea for this came about in the aftermath of the great success we had with our initial backpack giveaway. Everyone seemed to be feeling so good about that program that we just kind of assumed that we would get 100 percent participation from the entire company for a similar program going forward. "We thought there was no way any employee would resist this," says Scott. "It would be crazy to think someone wouldn't want to participate in the Culture of Good."

Wrong.

What we found was that even though we empowered our stores by giving them a Culture of Good budget and the ability to take two days off to volunteer to keep the momentum going, things actually kind of ebbed. What we recognized was that we made things really easy for everyone with the backpack giveaway: all they had to do was hand out good stuff to kids and their families. Done.

But now that we were asking them to start tackling some projects on their own, getting everyone on board was much harder. Yes, some people in some stores were very eager to carry the flag forward. But that wasn't the case everywhere. We began to bang our heads against the wall because people seemed to quickly revert back to the same old, same old: if it wasn't in their job description, they didn't have to do it. So we began to talk about ways that we could try to drive up participation throughout the company.

But how could we do that? We knew that if we went out there and said something like, "You guys aren't participating, and you are in serious trouble," that would kill off everything right then and there. Similarly, if we tried to single out the people who were slacking and punish them in some way as an example to everyone else, that wouldn't work either. We even tried an incentive program of sorts, where we would award free phones to the stores that racked up the largest number of donations from their customers. That failed because we rigged the incentives the wrong way: one store manager encouraged employees to make a large number of 1-cent donations as a way to stuff the ballot (we were then forced to let that manager go).

Ultimately, we decided to embrace a lesson from every leadership and parenting manual out there by finding ways to praise and lavish attention on the people who had embraced the Culture of Good. In particular, we identified people around the country who were super active in their community efforts and began to call them Champions. The idea was simple: we wanted to reward those employees who were most enthusiastic about the Culture of Good and empower them to spread their magic to everyone else in their stores. Since Ryan couldn't be present everywhere, the idea was for Champions to become "mini Ryans," if you will, where they could keep the fires of the Culture of Good stoked all the time across the company.

"I wanted us to hit the ground running from day one at 1,000 miles an hour," says Ryan. "But everyone was so busy in the whirlwind of work that I tried to do it all myself like I always had. But I eventually got to the point where I recognized that the movement we were trying to create wouldn't go anywhere if I didn't get consistent help from the people who were emotionally invested in what we were trying to do. We needed it to be more than me."

The Champions program was intended to create leaders out in the field who would be involved with Ryan in helping dream up, create, and then launch all of the initiatives that we had on the drawing board. We went looking for the people who had a passion for volunteerism and connecting our company to the communities we operated in. The people who told us they had the greatest passion for their communities were given the honor of becoming our first Champions. While that sounded good on paper, we ended up missing a big part of the equation when it came to hitting the sweet spot of the Culture of Good.

One individual in particular personified the mistake we made. Let's call him Champ. Ryan first heard about Champ from other people in the company who were talking about how Champ was so active in community efforts and was always e-mailing people to get them excited about what was coming up next. The Culture of Good clearly ran through his veins. When Ryan met Champ at a sales rally, Champ wasted no time in declaring, "I will have your job some day."

This was music to Ryan's ears! This was exactly the kind of person we needed out in the field to amplify Ryan's efforts. Only, he actually wasn't.

Why? Because as time went on and as Champ tried to do more and more good in the community, his performance at work began to slack off, badly. Eventually, a district manager called Ryan to let him know that Champ wasn't working out. While his heart was in the right place in terms of the community, the manager told Ryan, he wasn't performing in his job. His peers didn't respect him. And eventually he stopped showing up for work on time or even at all. Worse, he was blaming his poor performance on the time he was spending on his work for the Culture of Good. In short, he had gone way out of balance and was eventually let go.

That was a huge learning experience for us—and somewhat of a wake-up call. "Our takeaway was that you can't just have passion for doing good," says Scott. "You have to perform in your job. It's about finding that balance where you are also accountable to your peers and making sure that everyone in the company knows you care about each other as much as you care about the community."

Fortunately, we built on the lessons learned from the failed Champions program to implement a new rebranded program that we now call our Ambassador program. Ambassadors are nominated, recruited, and selected among our employees for their passionate belief in the Culture of Good. That means that they need to demonstrate how they believe that employees and customers matter as much as our cause, community matters, does in their everyday jobs. To help kick off that program in 2015, we hosted Passion, a two-day Ambassador event in Indianapolis where we focused on our evolving vision for the Culture of Good. Ryan and Peter Wallace, our former manager of communications for the Culture of Good, led the event.

The first day of Passion included keynote speeches from those who are most heavily involved in the Culture of Good, including Scott; Conrad Edwards, TCC's chief marketing officer; Peter; Ryan; and special guests such as Brian Layer, an executive with N2Growth, a professional services firm that assists in improving leadership in companies, and assistant vice president of corporate partnerships at Riley Hospital, Jim Austin. The discussions explained the why, how, and what of the Ambassador program. Essentially, we wanted to push our Ambassadors to think about how they could best set themselves and their stores up for success.

On the second day, Ryan, Peter, and all Ambassadors volunteered at Gleaners Food Bank of Indiana. The group of more than 100 participants was one of the largest groups of volunteers Gleaners ever welcomed through its doors. It was definitely a highlight of the event. Putting words into action and witnessing the happiness that volunteering brought to the Ambassadors that day were priceless. Consider this e-mail we got from a newly minted Ambassador afterward:

> *I just wanted to personally e-mail you and just say thank you (and the rest of your team) so much for the experience of Passion 2015. I am still pretty new with TCC and cannot express to you how thankful I am to be a part of a good company like this and surrounded by so many good people. I have never had this much of a sense of fulfillment from a job and cannot put into words how excited I am to take this and run with it. Thank you!*

More recently, we got a personal note from a newly minted Ambassador by the name of Blake Garner, who, when asked by a friend if he got paid more for volunteering in that role, said that he was paid more—in "feels."

The power of the Ambassador program is also the credibility that gets added in when you see your peers—and not just the boss—buying into the benefits of doing all that good and getting all those "feels." To that point, Mike Gephart, a sales manager from our store in Auburn, Indiana, sent us the following note about the importance of the Ambassador program:

> *Ryan!*
>
> *How's it goin', my good man?*
>
> *I would like to take a quick minute to put a spotlight on our COG Ambassador, Kattina Hantz. Her passion and guidance are freaking amazing. Allow me to paint a (hopefully) quick picture for you.*
>
> *First of all, for this story to make sense, you should know that Kattina is my fiancé and we have an amazing son together and she has changed my life. With that being said, I'm the manager of the Auburn store. We had a lot of problems with buy-in (for COG) at this location. Part of the problem was me. What turned out to be the main cause of this lack of buy-in was simply . . . knowledge. We didn't understand the logistics of COG. The whens and the hows.*
>
> *But then Kattina came to the store one day and gave us a step-by-step breakdown of everything. When to pick our new cause and when to donate. The difference between what we pick and the quarterly initiative—everything. This made me realize that original rollout of COG didn't filter down properly (I wasn't a manager at the time).*
>
> *Long story short, you should be happy for two reasons. (1) Auburn is now lit up and we're collecting donations at*

an awesome rate and everyone in the store is excited about it.
(2) You have an exceptional ambassador. She RADIATES
passion for this. She lives it.

   Thank you for changing our company. We needed it.
Mike Gephart

Getting this kind of feedback from folks such as Mike is huge in that it shows us how you really need to get the Culture of Good to spread. Obviously, when you have as many stores and locations as we do, Ryan can't be everywhere at once. Similarly, hearing about how the initiatives work via e-mail compared to having someone explain it to you in person while he or she RADIATES passion, well, the difference is obvious. We're sure we'll continue to build and improve on the Ambassador program based on feedback we get from people such as Kattina, which is exciting.

By tapping into the people such as Kattina, who Scott calls our "Jedis," those universally respected employees who are really the heart of our business, we think we could have ramped up the reasoning behind the Culture of Good much faster. We also could have asked the Jedis what ideas they wanted to pursue rather than asking them to jump on board programs that came from us, especially since we now have hundreds of Culture of Good initiatives being spearheaded by TCC employees throughout the year. This would have helped create an enormous amount of buy-in and engagement much earlier than we experienced.

Questions to Consider
Scott's Questions:

1.   How do you involve your people in how your organization operates? Are there opportunities to give them a greater voice in how things might be run better?

2. Be honest: are there people inside your organization today who just don't fit your culture? If so, why are you afraid to let them go?

3. Are your employees completely aware of your core beliefs and the company's vision and strategy, and can they talk to your customers about them?

Ryan's Questions:

1. What word or phrase would you use to describe the future of your organization or the company you work for? Ask your people or peers the same question and see how their answers compare to yours.

2. Have you tried to force or compel your people or have you been forced to do good deeds such as volunteer or donate money? What do you think you learned from those experiences?

Making Customers Better

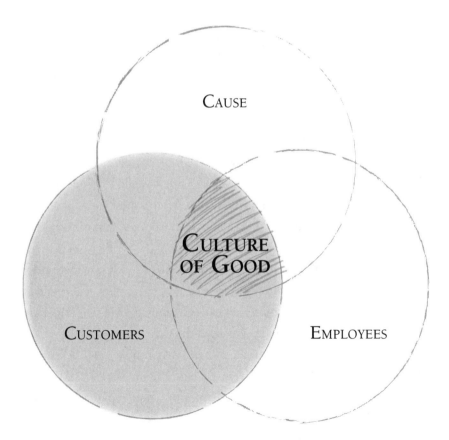

Now that we've talked about how causes and employees matter, the missing link in that equation keeping us from hitting the sweet spot at the center of the Culture of Good is our customers. Sure, this has some degree of overlap with our cause, since customers are also members of our communities. But by supporting the people in the communities where our stores are located, we can make a difference in the lives of the people our company touches. And that gives us opportunities to cement our ties with our customers and to reinforce **why** we do **what** we do. That serves as the basis for a value proposition you can share with your customers: that by buying your products or services, you are making the world a better place. If someone was on the fence before about doing business with you, learning that should make building a sustainable relationship with him or her a no-brainer.

That's why when we talk about making customers better, we're not referring to some newfangled customer service program. You can't run a successful business if you don't do things like customer service; that's just the ante to get into the game. Yes, you have to be maniacal about providing exceptional customer service. But that's not enough. Our goal here is to engage our customers in a multitude of ways and show them how they are directly contributing to all of the outcomes from the Culture of Good when they visit our stores. Today, 91.5 percent of TCC's employees mention our Culture of Good regularly when interacting with our customers, while 70 percent of our stores have gained new customers as a result of efforts to give back to our communities. As a result, TCC's customer base has increased 133 percent since we started the Culture of Good.

Admittedly, this remains an area where we continue to work hard to improve. And some of the initiatives we are putting in place at the time of the writing of this book might not pay off until after copies of it roll off the printer. For example, we're working hard to have videos and pictures in our stores that allow our customers to see all the good we can accomplish

106

because of their business. We are also creating ways to get our customers' input when it comes to the kinds of Culture of Good projects we undertake and which organizations we make donations to. The point is that we can't hit the sweet spot of the Culture of Good without our customers. The key is getting them to understand how they play such a critical role in helping us hit that mark.

Striking up Connections

To keep the Culture of Good alive, all of our associates should essentially think about our customers as more than just people we transact with or who buy stuff from us. Our customers choose us, which means we need to choose to understand how to best connect with them and help them understand the kind of impact they make with every purchase. They are people who have needs we can address. The technology we sell can make their lives easier, but only when it makes sense to them. In short, our goal is to create raving fans by becoming their trusted advisors. And we do that by "creating a welcoming atmosphere where we are honest and value the needs of our customers more than the need to complete a sale," says Kristy Barney, a 10-year TCC veteran who is now in charge of training the next generation of leaders inside our company. So how do we create that kind of welcoming atmosphere in our stores? Let us explain by first asking a question: how intimidated are you by technology?

Maybe you are someone who is an early adapter: you know, the kind of person who orders a new phone or gadget every six to nine months because you love the new features. You might even spend an inordinate amount of your free time reading up on consumer technology and may consider yourself something of an expert on the subject. If that's you, you might not think twice about ordering your next phone online, or, if you do go into a store, you beeline right for the product you have your sights set on. And that's awesome.

But most of our customers don't fall into that category. Our customers tend to find technology intimidating. That's why they'd rather come visit one of our stores to get advice on what they need than scroll through reams of unreliable online reviews. That means our people feel some pressure to deliver the goods. They need to be ready to really help people with something that's truly dear to them: their ability to communicate with their friends, families, and loved ones. And if you've ever lost your phone for any amount of time, you know that's no joke. That's why it's so essential for our people to adopt the mentality of thinking about what it's like to be walking in our customers' shoes: what can we do to help them? And we mean that. This isn't about scamming customers into buying more or faking interest in their needs. When we look at business history, so many businesses clearly fail when they lose track of their customers' needs and begin to prioritize the value of a single transaction instead.

A story worth sharing along those lines comes from Mugi Amu, a sales representative from our store in Lewisburg, Pennsylvania. Mugi, who joined TCC back in 2012, is such a great example of the kind of attitude we hope all of our associates bring with them into work each day. While Mugi has experienced tragedy in his own life—he and his wife have lost five children to illness—he says he found his passion by connecting deeply and personally with his customers on a daily basis. As he puts it:

> *It didn't take me long to realize that TCC is the place I wanted to be. I felt that TCC offers more than just an environment to exceed monthly goals but a place for ME to be myself. A place for me to take time, do it right, and be passionate about what I do because every day, I am interacting with strangers—whom we call CUSTOMERS! I realized our customers have wireless needs, they have families, they experienced loss of a loved one, they are celebrating birthdays, they are afflicted with incurable sicknesses, or they are getting married soon,*

*and the lists goes on. I learned a long time ago that money will
come if I take time to do good with my customers. I wanted
to do something different that separates me from others. And
I do that by SIMPLY LISTENING TO MY CUSTOMERS
DIFFERENTLY.*

"Simply listening to my customers differently and building friendships
beyond the sales floor mean far more to me than a commission check," says
Mugi. "TCC grants me the place and the opportunity to do more than
just selling every day. I strive to build a long-lasting friendship with my
customers because they matter to me—their stories, their lives, families,
and communities. That is what makes me love my job. Some day, I know
in my heart, they will come back and wait in line for me, and if I am not at
the store, my coworkers will get the business because I have done my job
right and fair! That is my calling."

That's why if you don't want to lose touch with the soul of your business, you need to encourage your people to spark genuine conversations
with each customer to make the connections that ultimately lead your
customers to understand their role in building a Culture of Good.

So how do we go about striking up connections like those Mugi made?
We begin with being intentional about how we interact with customers
from the very first minute they walk into one of our stores. That's part of
what we call the "Six Keys" that we train all of our sales associates on.

These Six Keys can be summed as first thanking the guests as soon as
they walk in and then engaging and connecting with them at a personal
level, which allows us to discover their lifestyle needs and suggest person-
alized solutions to address those needs. Finally, every conversation should
conclude with a tour of the store, which is an opportunity to talk to our
customers about the Culture of Good and why we do what we do. We can
share stories about how, by giving us their business, our customers are giving back to their communities. We get to explain how a percentage of every

sale goes to initiatives such as the backpack giveaway and the Teachers Rock initiative, for example. Or, how by purchasing an extra awesome cloth featuring the artwork of rocking kids such as Olivia, they are also helping fulfill the mission of the Culture of Good. "We're trying to create relationships with our customers and not just sell them a product," says Kristy, who just so happens to have been named TCC's employee of the year in 2015. "Our goal right from when those customers walk into one of our stores is to get to know them and their lifestyle as a way to help address their needs."

Sara Williams, a field director at TCC who oversees 26 different stores, says that when our sales associates can make the connection for customers about how the money they spend in the store or that they donate goes right back into the community, you start to see the lightbulbs pop on as they begin to understand their role in hitting the sweet spot at the center of the Culture of Good. "They get excited because they know the money is staying local," says Sara. "Everyone is always asking you to donate to this and that, but you don't know where it's really going. When we take the time to explain our cause, it starts a conversation."

Case in point: Jack Bainter is a TCC store manager in Bonaire, Georgia. He also happens to be our Atlanta region's Culture of Good Ambassador, people we charge with carrying on the movement and reinforcing the Culture of Good throughout the company. He shared a story with us about a Habitat for Humanity event his team participated in to help build a new house for a family in need. After they started working on the project, the lead contractor approached Jack on site, so he stopped working to have a conversation with the man. Here's what happened next in Jack's words:

> *The contractor started by telling us how much he appreciated our efforts and the $125 donation that we made to help support the project. Then he said, "You're Jack, right? You helped me and my wife get our new phones and transfer all of our*

information to the new phones." He went on to tell me how awesome our store and customer service are and that he had never had a joyful experience purchasing a new phone. I took the time with them to tell them about our Culture of Good and that we give back to the local community. They liked the information and thought it was great that we did that as such a large organization. It wasn't until we showed up on their actual work site that the impact of our Culture of Good was real to our customers. He was amazed at the work we put in and even took the time to talk to our leadership people who came and let them know what a great job we did and how he was impressed with our company's efforts to help our local communities. He went on to say that he and his wife would be spreading the word and would be sending as many people our way as possible.

Another great example of how we use conversations about the Culture of Good to support and fuel the notion of how we make the connection between our customers and our communities comes from Jess Combs, a sales associate in Seymour, Indiana, who has personally raised hundreds of dollars, usually $1 or $2 at a time, just by striking up conversations with our customers and helping them connect to the goals of the Culture of Good. Not surprisingly, Jess has also sold dozens of awesome cloths because of her ability to speak passionately about how a customer's contribution impacts children's lives. "I let them know the awesome things we do within the community with their donation and that this isn't just a 10 percent contribution like you see from other businesses," says Jess.

To that very end, we started a new nonprofit at the time we were finishing writing this book, called TCC Gives, as a way to help hit that sweet spot in the Culture of Good by giving out grants to local charities selected by our employees and customers. Scott's wife, Julie, who just happens to be pursuing a master's degree in philanthropic studies from the prestigious Lilly Family School of Philanthropy in Indianapolis, will head up the organization once it gets rolling, about the time that this book comes out.

Julie and Scott actually started the Moorehead Family Foundation, which we mentioned earlier in the book, as a way to create a more formal process for sharing profits from TCC with good causes, particularly in Marion, where the company got started. But Julie saw an opportunity to expand awareness of how the company gives back not just in Indiana but also across the country wherever a TCC store might be. She wanted to give every employee at TCC the chance to give back to our cause of community matters in meaningful ways, in the way she and Scott had been able to do in Marion.

"That's why we decided to rebrand and change the name," says Julie. "And we created a 501(c)3 as a way to get more freedom to do the things we want to do."

The driver behind TCC Gives, Julie says, will be "sponsors," or employees who will submit requests for grants to support their favorite causes. By doing that, TCC will be "able to support what our employees support," says Julie, adding that the money involved with TCC Gives will be separate from the COG budgets each store already gets to spend. Even better, our goal is that our employees will team up with our customers to pursue the kinds of causes that they are jointly most passionate about. That's how we can hit the mark at the center of the Culture of Good by bringing together our employees and our customers with our community.

For example, let's say a TCC employee named Jack loved our Heal the Earth Day event. Jack then got to talking to the manager at the local community park that day and realized they were looking for $5,000 to add some public benches. Jack felt so good about cleaning up spaces like this and saw a real need for these benches. With TCC Gives, Jack can now go to the manager at the parks group and tell him that they can now apply for a grant together. And to do that, all they have to do is go online and fill out the grant, easy peasy. If the committee in charge of handing out those grants likes the idea as much as Jack does, then he gets the money for the benches. Just as importantly, Jack has also created a new relationship with the park manager, who might just become a customer as well.

Another example might involve Tony, a local guy who volunteers regularly with the Boys and Girls Club. Let's say that Tony comes into his local TCC store and he sees on the walls that "Community Matters." So he asks Sarah, the store manager, what that means exactly. By sharing what the folks at her store do to support the kids in the community, Sarah learns how passionate Tony is about those same issues. So Sarah suggests that she and Tony fill out a grant application together to help their Boys and Girls Club since she knows firsthand how much this organization positively impacts kids' lives. And a new relationship between an employee and a customer linked by their love of their community is formed at the same time. That's a beautiful thing because it truly ties together all of the elements of the Culture of Good symbiotically.

Questions to Consider
Scott's questions:

1. If you could connect your customers to your cause, would that be a value proposition for your company?

2. If your customers knew nothing else about your business beyond your cause, would that move the bar for you with them?

3. Are you aware of another company's cause proposition, and did you connect with it? Why or why not? Did it come across as disingenuous?

Ryan's questions:

1. What is the most compelling reason for customers to do business with you?

2. In what ways are you introducing your customers to your company culture so they know where they fit into it?

3. How convinced are your customers that your cause is authentic, and what are you doing to communicate that to them?

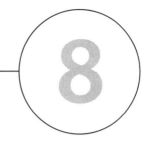

Finding Your
Company's Soul

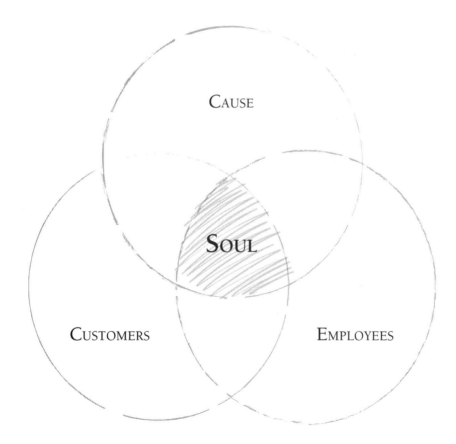

CAUSE

SOUL

CUSTOMERS

EMPLOYEES

It's crazy to think back about the journey we've been on over the past few years and how we have fulfilled those intentions we set at the start of it. And that's the beauty of making the time to write this book together. We've had the chance to press pause, even just briefly, to reflect on the culture Scott's parents started and what we have built on together with our associates. Writing this book has given us the opportunity to truly appreciate how we came to build a thriving culture and to find our company's soul again. Our hope is that you have found our story inspiring enough for you to begin asking the questions that can spark a Culture of Good in your company.

Another reason writing this book has been a valuable experience for us is that it's helped us recognize how lucky we were to discover the power of encouraging people to bring their soul to work with them when you build a Culture of Good. We almost seemed to stumble down the right path by following our collective gut instincts. We have made our share of mistakes along that journey, as we have shared with you. After all, change is hard—especially change on the scale of rewiring a fast-growing company's culture with thousands of people working in it all over the country. We were very fortunate that, in the end, we found what we were looking for, even though we maybe didn't always know where we were headed.

Drawing attention to yourself and the supposed good deeds that you do can feel disingenuous. It almost defeats the purpose of doing good in the first place if everyone else thinks you're doing it only to get extra credit.

But here's another thought to chew on: what happens if nobody shares the good things that people are doing? What if that kind of vacuum leads us to believe all of the horribly negative stories that we are blasted with so often? Is it possible that we could all stand to share more of the good stories as a way to inspire others to do similar things—to embrace the idea of doing good better? Would that be a threat to our authenticity and turn people off?

Maybe. Certainly, we have many employees at TCC who never needed to be given time to go volunteer or do good: they were already doing things all along. But for those of us who needed to be given permission to think about doing good at work, perhaps we all need to think more about sharing the good we are collectively accomplishing as a way to inspire others to do something similar. And you don't need to build a Culture of Good on your own before you can start sharing and inspiring.

Building something like we did was really an act of what we call in business parlance "change management"—which is not always the easiest thing to pull off in an established company. It all comes down to how you get people to change the way they are used to doing things and remain engaged with their work along the way. It ain't always easy, that's for sure. But the impact is undeniable.

Consider the answers we got back when we asked a group of employees who have been with TCC for a while to describe what the Culture of Good means to them using only a single sentence:

- A lifestyle about leaving the world a better place than you found it.

- A group of people truly engaged in doing good in our community because it's the right thing to do.

- TCC believes in community, employees, and customers, and we use the Culture of Good as the vehicle to help those in need in the communities we touch.

- An incredible initiative that leverages our company's assets to give back to our community.

- Business and employees having an impact on community, people, and self.

- A great movement that instills positivity to all around it.

- You have the ability to make a difference outside of your four walls.

- Making good intentions intentional.

- We've found our opportunity to change the world; want in?

How do you think your employees would describe your culture in a single sentence? Would they embrace a Culture of Good? If so, what does that mean for you and finding your company's sweet spot? What do you need to change to get there?

If you Google the phrase "culture change," you will find hundreds of links to so-called experts on the subject. Many of these folks have written books on the subject that offer up practical tips on how you go about implementing the nitty-gritty details of cultural change in a business. They tell you, step by step, how to make it happen. But there's something missing. Few, if any, of these folks actually tell you what your end goal is. They don't know how to help you define what kind of culture you should have.

Scott remembers listening to a podcast that featured one of these culture change experts talking about her eight-step program to changing culture. But when the interviewer asked her about what she was trying to accomplish in going though that change, the woman totally stumbled. She was great at defining the *how* of culture change, but she didn't understand *what* the real goal was or *why* someone should do it.

That actually became an aha moment for us because what this expert was missing was the idea that culture change is really about finding your company's soul—which, for us, is that inner circle where your cause, your employees, and your customers intersect. That's where every business's special sauce—your core values and beliefs—exists. That's why, if you want to build a Culture of Good, you need to embrace the idea that you are implementing a new operating system for your business rather than a set of independent programs. If all you do is start new or improve existing programs, you'll find that you're just treating symptoms rather than the root cause you're really after.

Building Your Culture of Good

Now that you have read our book, some of you may want to go further and consider implementing the Culture of Good in your own organization. First understand that the Culture of Good is at once generative and regenerative. When employees know they are valued, they transmit that value to their peers and customers.

The principle that propels the Culture of Good gives employees the *permission to care*. From that sense of care emerges a commitment and a passion to contribute to a greater good.

The Culture of Good can be taught to purposeful businesses that want to engage more deeply with their employees, customers, and cause in order to effect positive change.

So where should you begin?

1. Identify Your Cause

Ask yourself what you are passionate about. Consider what you could do to make a positive difference in the world. At TCC, our cause is community. Yours may be the same or something different. The challenge for you is to select a cause that you know would involve your people.

Now ask yourself the following questions:

1.   Does your cause align with your company's strategic vision?

2.   How is it authentic?

3.   Why does it matter to your employees?

4.   Why does it matter to your customers?

2. Connect It to Your Employees

Your cause will be sustainable only if it involves the hearts and minds of your people. First, look for ways to explain what you want to accomplish. Attack the mind. Build a plan for reaching out to your people. This means you must communicate, communicate, communicate. Engage their hearts by giving them something to experience. At TCC, the backpack giveaway was our first major experience. It captured the hearts of our people. Keep in mind that communications and experiences must be ongoing. Once is not enough. Determine a cadence of communications and experiential events that suits your organization best.

Now consider the following questions:

1. How will you build your plan for how your employees can connect to your cause?

2. How will you weave your cause into how you interview, hire, onboard, train, retain, inspire, and compensate?

3. What will you do to continue to communicate the cause to your employees?

4. What will you do to ensure that employees have permission to care so they can discover their calling?

3. Connect Your Cause to Your Customers

Customers can play an essential role in your cause. Research shows that consumers patronize businesses that share their same values. In this regard, they are similar to employees who choose to work at companies with values that mirror their own. Encourage customers to become involved by making it comfortable for them to participate. Let them know what your cause is and why it is important to your organization and its employees. At TCC, we let our customers know that a percentage of every sale goes to support a community event. This communication is the first step in engaging the customer in your cause. It can lead the way to building a stronger relationship between your organization and your customers that improves customer retention and creates greater awareness for your cause.

Now consider the following questions:

1. How can you use your culture and your cause to gain and retain customers?

2. How can you encourage your employees to take pride in telling your customers about your cause?

3. What can you communicate to your customers to let them know they have a role to play in fulfilling your cause?

Benefits of Hindsight

It's never truly as simple as following a three-step process. Very few business book authors admit that shit. We've had the benefits of living this process, and we know you'll stumble—just don't make the same mistakes we did.

When we look back at the journey we have taken since we kicked off the Culture of Good movement inside our company without the benefit of someone laying out the steps above, it's kind of crazy that it all works. Seriously. We didn't always know what we were doing, and perhaps without the success of the initial backpack giveaway, we might not have the ammunition and credibility to be writing this book today. Fortunately, we pulled it off—largely because, as we've said all along, we started doing it because it just felt like the right thing to do. Our authenticity went a long way with our ability to build trust and credibility with our team members, so that, even when we screwed up, the whole thing didn't collapse like a house of cards. We've now moved beyond taking individual initiatives and company events and have learned how to build the Culture of Good into our very DNA.

As we have said before, building the Culture of Good has been a learning experience for us right from the start. We have had to adjust as we've moved along while rebounding from efforts that didn't produce the kinds of end results we thought they would.

One major adjustment in our understanding of the Culture of Good system is that we identified that we initially implemented the process without knowing the proper order. Had we done things in the order we have shared in this book and introduced the operational system to all of our existing systems, teams, and leaders, then we could have significantly reduced the time it took to begin seeing its impact on our company. We now see what it takes to build a Culture of Good and with confidence recognize that our missteps along the way may have turned us into culture experts.

But that also begs an important question that we get asked a lot by people and companies who have heard our story: **Does my company need soul brothers like Scott and Ryan to make this work for us?**

The short answer is yes. By that, we don't mean that you need one of us to come work for your company (though we'll listen to any offers) as much as you need someone in your organization who believes in the power of the Culture of Good and will keep the fires stoked over time. Ryan likes to say he's like a pebble in the shoes of everyone who works at TCC: that little thing that you can't ignore no matter how much you might try. With each step you take, it's there to remind you to remember why you are tackling whatever it is you might be doing.

We'd also say it's essential to have buy-in from the top leadership in the organization for this to really take hold. You need the folks who make the key decisions for the organization to believe in their hearts that this is a crucial component to the organization's success. If they aren't ready to support this kind of movement with resources and mental energy, well . . . you get the picture.

But what else can we learn from our experience with the Culture of Good in terms of what we did right and what we would do differently? Or, with the benefit of hindsight, what tips can we share that might be helpful as you undergo your own journey? We'll do our best to address those questions below. But if we somehow fail to touch on something you're interested in, reach out to us via our website, cultureofgood.com, which is a thriving online community where people like you can connect with us and other likeminded companies. Like we said, this is becoming a movement!

Here are some additional lessons learned from our journey that might be helpful in making your own Culture of Good adventure even more fulfilling and engaging for your organization.

Tap the Wisdom of the Crowd

As we shared earlier in the book, we began our Culture of Good journey as a dynamic duo. With Scott's support, Ryan did most of the heavy lifting early on based on his years of experience working for his church and other nonprofits. But TCC was Ryan's first experience working in a for-profit organization, and each and every day proved to be a learning experience in making connections and how to communicate the plans that we were hatching together in Scott's office. While this allowed us to make decisions quickly, it also wasn't perfect. Simply e-mailing people around the country wasn't all that effective at getting the word out about what the Culture of Good was and WHY we were trying to do what we were doing. That works well when you're running an organization with 100 people or so based in a single location.

If we had it to do over, we would have done a couple of things differently. For one, we would have brought in several layers of leadership in the company to get them bought in as early as possible. In our case, we didn't set up regular update meetings with leaders until two years after the debut of the Culture of Good. It would have been very helpful to have leaders in the different areas of the company, such as marketing, sales, or operations, on board to help explain what our goals were right from the beginning. Similarly, it would have been greatly helpful to have tapped into the ideas and suggestions from those leaders about what they thought we might do to get off to the best possible start while also helping us sustain our movement over the long term.

Prioritize Communication

There's no doubt we also could have done a more effective job of using additional tools and techniques to get the word out about the Culture of Good across the company. We could have established a more official online strategy, for example, perhaps by including more information on the company's main site rather than on a separate web page.

We also would have set up a shared calendar as a way for everyone inside the company to see what events were happening around the country at any given time. This is important because it becomes a way to let everyone know what's going on and to pick up ideas from each other. Plus, it could even inspire some folks from different stores to visit and participate in their events. Now, any time one of our Ambassadors sets up an event at his or her store, it generates an e-mail blast that gets sent out to the rest of the company as well as to the shared calendar.

We also could have had a better communication plan in place to connect with our customers about what we were trying to do—more than just handing them a fortune cookie (though we still think that produced some pretty good results). After all, customers are one of the key components of our Culture of Good.

Automate, Automate, Automate

Scott has always been a big believer in the notion that if you want to improve something, you need to track and measure it. That applies to the

Culture of Good as well. Specifically, we track the number of hours that our people log in terms of their volunteer time. We've also had to learn to define and create new metrics for tracking things such as community engagement. While it's great to have people active and involved in the community, we also need to track and measure something beyond feel-good stories. After all, the plural of anecdote is not data.

We have set goals for what we would like to accomplish as an organization, so we track our progress along those lines. We also track other metrics, such as the amount of food we donate through our stores as well as money we raise for local charities. Well, what we didn't take into account was how much time it can take to track all of that information if you ask people to keep tabs manually. In the beginning, for instance, we had our people filling out paper forms to log volunteer hours per store, which Ryan then had to scan and digitize to enter those figures into our database. As we continued to ramp up, Ryan needed to add a full-time staff person just to deal with all that data entry, which sometimes took up to two weeks out of every month! That was a lot of wasted time that could have been better invested in doing good somewhere.

Fortunately, we learned our lesson and have found ways to automate much of that data entry by using shared online databases such as Salesforce. com as a tool to enter data and produce reports. The lesson here is that you, too, should embrace automation like this early on in your Culture of Good rollout.

Plan Long Term

Like many of the aspects of the Culture of Good, we often acted opportunistically and in the moment. If there was a chance to do good, we took it. But with hindsight, we can now more easily see that everyone would have benefited if we had taken a more long-term approach to planning our different events and initiatives as a way to help our people feel like this was something that was going to last, that it wasn't just a flavor of the month. Rather than launching event after event, we could have helped people get into a cadence and plan their own working and personal lives months in advance.

Pulling It All Together

All of the lessons we've learned in our journey together over the past few years hit close to home recently when we had a friend come to us asking for help in creating his own Culture of Good. He was amazed by what he saw happening in our company, and he wanted to energize his own business in a similar way. The experience was fascinating for us to be welcomed into his business with an eye on helping him kick off his own culture-change efforts. But rather than embarrass our friend within the pages of this book, we turned his story into a parable of sorts to help share the lessons we learned from our visit.

The hero of our story is named Lyle. He's a CEO of a manufacturing factory located on the East Coast. The company is very good at what it does, which is making fire extinguishers. You know, the kind you might have under your kitchen sink. Lyle's company made the best fire extinguishers in the business. When someone needed to put out a fire, those extinguishers worked every time. They saved lives. Because of that good reputation, there was demand for Lyle's products around the country, which helped his company earn enough profit to keep churning out more fire extinguishers.

But something was missing. When Lyle showed up at the factory every day, his employees didn't seem engaged in their work. Sure, they got the job done. But that was all they did: nothing less and nothing more. They collected their paycheck and then went home. Morale seemed to be low for some reason, but Lyle couldn't figure out why. When he tried sending out an employee satisfaction survey, he found that few, if anybody, felt truly engaged in their job. As a result, Lyle lost some skilled people he couldn't afford to lose. Worse, no matter how many ads he placed or recruiters he called, he couldn't seem to fill those positions again with qualified candidates. Meanwhile, the people he did hire just didn't seem to have the same passion for the business that Lyle did.

Over time, as the quality of his people began to erode, so, too, did the loyalty of the company's customers—especially the buyers from the retail stores who liked to come and visit the factory from time to time. It was almost like they could tell something was missing as well. So they soon began to place their orders elsewhere. When Lyle would call these key customers to find out why they didn't place their order, he was told that the place didn't have the same energy that it used to.

To his credit, Lyle tried everything he could to turn things around. He started by investing in some new equipment, figuring people would appreciate having the best tools to work with. He outfitted a break room with a kitchen and a couch for people to relax on during their breaks. He even started a customer loyalty program where he would award a company-wide bonus for customers who increased their orders. Lyle also felt it was important to give to a cause. So every year, after he closed the books, he would write a nice check and donate it to a national organization that supported fallen firefighters. He would then take a picture of that check and post it in the break room so that everyone in the company would know that their hard work was also doing some good in the world.

And doing good was something Lyle was passionate about away from work as well. Not only did he donate to both national and local causes on his own but also he volunteered during his free time. He especially enjoyed the experience of volunteering through a program at his local fire station where they would go help install smoke detectors in people's homes. Giving back to people in need was something he was passionate about. He knew that many of his employees gave back in their free time as well.

But whenever he tried to organize a walk to raise money for cancer or feed starving kids in another country, he heard crickets.

Even with all of Lyle's efforts, nothing changed. He realized that his culture was stuck in neutral. But he also didn't know how to kick it into gear—to take it from a Culture of OK to a Culture of Good.

This was the point where we showed up at Lyle's company. And, based on the experience of our journey, we knew within an hour how we could help Lyle and his employees begin to build a Culture of Good in his business. We knew how to help Lyle make his company an awesome place to work for and to buy from again. Now that you've read our story, the question is, do you? A good first step might be getting some chips and salsa.

Acknowledgments

Scott Moorehead

This book project wouldn't have been possible without the help, love, support, and persistent nagging of many people close to me. I cannot thank my wife, Julie, enough. She is without a doubt my angel sent to keep life on track. Mason and Marlee for being an inspiration for me to try to change the future of our world for the better. My parents, who trusted their "baby" with their nest egg. I still carry the same torch you passed me. My brother for consistently believing in me and being my business partner for life. The countless friends, team members, coaches, business partners, vendors, and peers who throughout my career have supported my personal "special kind of weird." Ryan McCarty, you are an inspiration to all walks of life—never change!!

Ryan McCarty

I wish to personally thank the following people for their contributions to my inspiration and knowledge and other help in creating this book: Darren Dahl for spending hundreds of hours listening and writing with us in spite of moments of perturbation; Pastor Bill Wilson for wrecking my life in the best way in 1993 with his message of "The need is the call"; Pastor James Bradley for giving me hope that there is always hope when I had almost given up; my wife, Katara, who makes me a better version of myself and gives me reasons every day to keep falling in love; my girls, Bria and Brenna, for giving me the joy and greatest calling of being their dad and for living this good in the world while refusing to live for money;

my parents, who instilled in me the belief that every person has value no matter what; each reader who will take this idea of the Culture of Good and make it reality for each company and organization across the world; Scott Moorehead, who keeps believing in me no matter how crazy he thinks my ideas are and challenges me that I can dream bigger if I'm willing to try; and, lastly, my six-year-old self, whose world collapsed around him in 1982 and yet continues to remind me every day why I do what I do. This book would not be without each of you.

About the Authors

Ryan McCarty and Scott Moorehead

Scott Moorehead has been a lifelong resident of Indiana. He fell for his future wife in high school and they set upon a journey of live music, travel, adventure, and raising their two kids. When Scott graduated from Purdue University, he vowed to never be typical in any business venture or challenge.

Ryan McCarty has always had a passion for making the world a better place. Ryan's wife and two daughters teamed up with the culture zealot to start a church, build a school in Africa, and launch an afterschool network that exists across states and even countries. Although Ryan would like to be an old-school hip-hop star, he spends his spare time listening to NPR and watching *Antique Roadshow* while smoking a pipe.